things to look for
when selecting a
C compiler
p. 109 - get line()
p.96 declare local
    variables in
compound statements
p 83 operators

No. 1873
$21.95

SUREFIRE
PROGRAMMING IN

WARREN A. STEWART

**A hands-on
introduction to
using C on CP/M, MS-DOS, *and*
Unix-based microcomputers!**

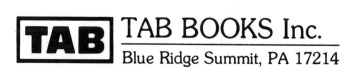

TAB BOOKS Inc.
Blue Ridge Summit, PA 17214

UNIX is a trademark of AT&T Bell Laboratories. CP/M is a trademark of Digital Research, Inc. MS-DOS, Xenix are trademarks of Microsoft. ZEUS is a trademark of Zilog. CROMIX is a trademark of CROMEMCO. Idris is a trademark of Whitesmiths LTD. Coherent is a trademark of Mark Williams Co. Unos is a trademark of Charles River Data Systems. PDP, DEC, and VAX, Ultrix are trademarks of Digital Equipment Corp. IBM, PCIX are trademarks of International Business Machines. ATT is a trademark of ATT. BDS C is a trademark of BD Software. C/80 and TOOLWORKS are trademarks of The Software Toolworks, and DeSMET C is a trademark of DeSmet Software.

FIRST EDITION

FIRST PRINTING

Copyright © 1985 by TAB BOOKS Inc.
Printed in the United States of America

Library of Congress Cataloging in Publication Data

Stewart, Warren A.
Surefire programming in C.

Bibliography: p.
Includes index.

1. C (Computer program language) I. Title.
QA76.73.C15S74   1985   001.64'24   84-26898
ISBN 0-8306-0873-7
ISBN 0-8306-1873-2 (pbk.)

Cover illustration by Larry Selman

Contents

Preface

In the media surrounding computer technology, UNIX and C have become familiar terms. Industry analysts assess the strategic importance of UNIX for AT&T in its battle with IBM for the computer marketplace. They monitor the reactions to the announcements of a growing number of UNIX clones—operating systems such as Coherent, Zeus, Idris, Xenix, Cromix, Unos, Pcix, and Ultrix, just to name a few.

The success of UNIX in the world of minicomputers is legendary. Briefly, UNIX began with Ken Thompson's work on a PDP-7 minicomputer in 1969. In a 1978 article, McIlroy reports that there was one overriding objective of the UNIX development—to create a computing environment in which programming research could comfortably and effectively take place (*Bell System Technical Journal*, July-August, 1978). From these beginnings, UNIX became a full-blown operating system for the Digital Equipment Corporation PDP/11 series of minicomputers.

The original UNIX was written in assembly language. The C programming language was designed by Dennis Ritchie of Bell Laboratories as a language in which to rewrite UNIX. Now the vast majority of the UNIX system and its application programs are written in C. For that matter, C is the primary programming language of the UNIX environment.

C is a general purpose language useful for a range of applications. It has been described as a low level language with high level data structures and control features. C is called low level because objects that are often manipulated in assembly language—bits, bytes, and machine addresses—can also be manipulated in C.

C is now a common language among microcomputer software developers. It is a fun language to use and a language whose base of users grows daily. This book is intended as an introduction to C. It is a language you can use for professional programming and hobby activities on your personal computer. I hope you find the introduction pleasurable.

Acknowledgments

Several people have made generous contributions toward my writing this book, and to all of them I am grateful. My thanks go to Walt Bilofsky, Susan Hayes, Leor Zolmon, Fredrick Richter, Rick Rump, Harvey Nero, and Mark Byrd for contributing C compilers and for helping solve various disk formatting problems encountered along the way.

Manuscript review comments by Denis Conrady and James Hunt significantly improved the book. Larry Freyou and Art Norton tested many of the programs on their computers. And Carol Lindsey's painstaking review of the manuscript and numerous editorial suggestions greatly improved the book.

Without my wife Ellen, this book would not have been possible. In addition to her editing skills and word processing prowess, her encouragement, understanding, and love sustained me throughout the project. To Ellen, my thanks and my love.

This book is dedicated to my parents:
Clarke D. and Josephine B. Stewart

Introduction

One writes a computer program to instruct a machine to perform a task. Because machines cannot communicate in natural languages like English, it is necessary to write the instructions in a language the computer can understand.

The computer's native language is composed of ones and zeros. A valid instruction in the computer's language might be 1011101111000001. These *words* are part of a binary language, a language in which only the symbols 0 and 1 are used. This binary word may tell the computer to perform an addition operation in one of its arithmetic registers. Clearly, writing thousands of these binary instructions yields a computer program difficult for humans to understand. Higher level programming languages were developed to serve as a middle ground. The C programming language is one such language.

This book is intended for those who want to learn to write in C. It is assumed that you have access to a C compiler and a computer system on which you can experiment with the programs shown in this book. C compilers are available from a variety of manufacturers for many different computer systems. There *is* some variation in the way the language has been implemented by different manufacturers. In addition to providing detailed information on the common features these implementations share, this book presents material and exercises that will help you discover the nonstandard features your compiler possesses. Further, guidelines are given as to how the programs in this book can be modified to properly execute with a nonstandard C compiler.

This book is a tutorial on writing programs in C; you need not be an expert programmer to use it. In some cases BASIC language programs are used for comparative purposes. Though little is lost if you are not familiar with BASIC, some familiarity with the terminology associated with programming languages is helpful.

Chapter 1 presents examples of elementary C programs and discusses the environment in which C programs are developed. The C preprocessor and some fundamental input/output operations are also discussed. Chapter 2 introduces variables, data types, constants, and arrays and indicates how each of the data types is printed.

In Chapter 3, the overall organization of a typical C program is discussed, the distinction between local variables and global variables is presented, and the concept of a C function is developed. Chapter 4 presents arithmetic and relational operators, while Chapter 5 introduces control statements.

Pointers and arrays are the topics of Chapter 6, structures are introduced in Chapter 7, and Chapter 8 is devoted to input and output (I/O) operations. Examples of programs that perform disk I/O for standard UNIX C and nonstandard C compilers are provided. Finally, Chapter 9 presents several advanced topics, including recursion, bit level operations, typedef statements, and unions.

Two appendices are also provided. Appendix A is for readers who are not familiar with the octal and hexadecimal number systems, or scientific notation. The appendix provides an overview of these topics. Appendix B is a series of tables that have been placed at the end of the book for easy reference.

NOTATION USED IN THIS BOOK

The ellipses(...) are used to mean "and so on." For example,

$$1,2,3, \ldots , 99$$

represents the first 99 positive integers.

References to other literature are cited by a bracketed indicator such as [KERN78], which refers to Kernighan and

Ritchie's definitive work on the C programming language. The list of references is found at the end of the book.

Some sections are marked with an asterisk (*). These sections can safely be skimmed or skipped on the first reading. You can return to these sections at a later point after gaining more familiarity with C. All other notation used is introduced in the text.

Chapter 1

Getting Started with C

To begin learning C, let's examine our first C program:

```
main() {
    /* A program to print welcome */

    printf("welcome");
}
```

If you are familiar with BASIC, you'll find this C program is just like the following BASIC program:

```
10 REM A PROGRAM TO PRINT WELCOME
20 PRINT "welcome"
```

Or, if you have programmed in Pascal, it is like the following Pascal program:

```
PROGRAM WELCOMEPROG (OUTPUT);
(* A PROGRAM TO PRINT WELCOME *)
BEGIN
    WRITELN('welcome')
END.
```

Because this is our first C program, let's examine it in some detail. *Main* is the name of a C *function*. Every C program has a

1

function called main. The parentheses following the word *main* indicate that it is a function. Functions are like black boxes of computation and logic. Data can be passed to them and they act on the data according to the instructions they contain. The main function of the welcome program is not passed any data; that is why there is nothing between the parentheses following its name. "C"

The left brace ({) introduces the statements that define the function main. This version of main begins with a comment. All text between the symbols /* and */ is commentary for the benefit of the programmer or other human readers. Following the comment, there is one statement:

```
printf("welcome");
```

Statements are written in a free format; they are not required to begin in a particular column, and more than one statement can be written on the same line.

Printf, like main, is a function. You can tell by the parentheses that follow its name. Between printf's parentheses are the characters "welcome". This string of seven characters (the double quotation marks are not included) is data that is passed to the function printf. Printf is a function that writes the data passed to it on the terminal screen.

The semicolon following printf("welcome") is the C statement terminator. Every C statement is terminated by a semicolon. Finally, the closing right brace (}) indicates the end of the statements in the function main. "}"

— like a the colon ; is use to seperate statements in basic

You have just examined your first C program. But, before you leave it, you should be aware that the first C program behaves a little differently than a first BASIC or Pascal program (as they are written here). The second C program points out the difference:

```
main() {
    /* This is your
            second C program */

    printf("hi");
    printf("there");
}
```

It may appear that this program will print two lines of text, but actually it prints only one line. The printf function does not

2

automatically move down a line each time it is used. If you want a new line, you must explicitly say so. Thus, the first program prints:

welcome

while the second program prints:

hithere

If the second program is intended to print two lines, the program would look like this:

```
main() {
        printf("hi\n");
        printf("there");
}
```

The \n is a special "escape sequence" used in C to represent a new line. C provides escape sequences for several invisible characters. A discussion of this and other C escape sequences is found in Chapter 2. Note that the comment in the second program extends across two lines. All text between /* and */ is a comment, even when the text spans two or more lines.

These programs are simple indeed; but to make them actually work on your system you must enter the program text into the system, and then *compile* and *link* the program. If you have used compilers before and are familiar with the process of compilation and linkage, skip forward to the section on the "C preprocessor" later in this chapter. If you are not familiar with the process, you should read the description that follows. In the next section, you will examine the type of environment that supports C programming.

THE C PROGRAMMING ENVIRONMENT

In the previous section you examined a couple of elementary C programs. Now, you will examine the process which transforms C language programs into executable machine code programs. The process has several distinct phases: program creation using a text editor, compilation, linkage editing, and debugging. The following sections highlight these phases of program development.

Text Editing and Compilation

The first step in writing a C program is to type the C statements into a file. A text editor is used to accomplish this task. The use of a text editor will not be discussed in this book; if you are not already accustomed to the text editor on your system, take a little time to familiarize yourself with its use.

The file containing C statements is called a *source file* or *source code*. Source files are translated into the machine code instructions that execute in the computer. The translation from source code to machine code is performed by a series of computer programs. The first translation program is the C compiler. A C compiler's job is to translate (or compile) C language statements into assembly language statements. Assembly language is a human readable form of machine code. The assembly language statements are then processed by the assembler. The assembler translates assembly language into object modules or object code. Figure 1–1 depicts the process of C program development discussed so far.

With the production of the object code, the translation from source code to machine code is nearly complete. However, several object files are required to make one executable program. For example, if your program uses the printf function, the object code for that function must become a part of your program. Various object files must be linked together to form one executable program. Thus, the last step in the translation process is to link object files into the final machine code. This task is performed by a program called a *linkage-editor* or *linker*.

The Linker

The linker allows previously compiled functions to be used in programs. This is an important feature of the C environment. It saves time; often-used functions do not have to be repeatedly

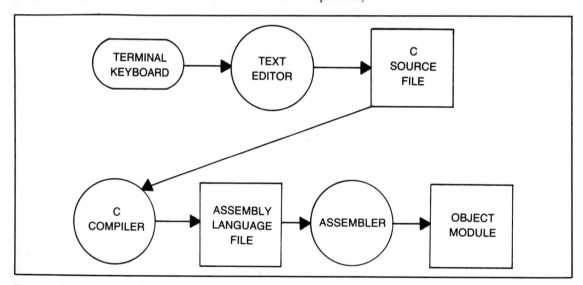

Fig. 1–1. C program development process: text editing and compilation.

4

recompiled. Further, compiler vendors will supply libraries of functions you can link into your programs. For example, functions such as printf, getchar, and putchar are supplied in input/output libraries and are readily available for your use. Such libraries let you create useful programs much more rapidly than if you had to write all the functions yourself.

In addition to linking vendor-supplied object code into your programs, you can use the linker to link functions you have developed into your programs. For instance, suppose you have written a C function to sort names alphabetically. It would be convenient if you could use this function in several programs without having to compile it on every occasion. You could generate the object code once, and use that code in several programs. Environments that support C generally allow this feature. This feature is called *separate compilation*. The linker is used to link separately compiled functions into one executable program.

Figure 1-2 updates Fig. 1-1 by adding the action of the linker and showing the resulting picture of the program development process.

Compile and Link Commands

The commands you issue on your system to perform compilation and linkage depend on the compiler you are using. As examples of how the command sequence appears, suppose you want to create an executable program from C source statements stored in a file called prog.c. Using the BDS C compiler, the commands would be:

```
cc prog.c
clink prog
```

The first command invokes the compiler. After the compilation is complete, the second command invokes the linker.

To perform the same process with the DeSmet C compiler on an IBM PC, the commands would be:

```
c88 prog.c
bind prog
```

Again, the compiler is invoked by the first command, and the linker is invoked by the second.

As you can see, the actual commands required to perform the compilation and linkage process vary from system to system. Refer to the user guide supplied with your compiler to determine the commands required on your system.

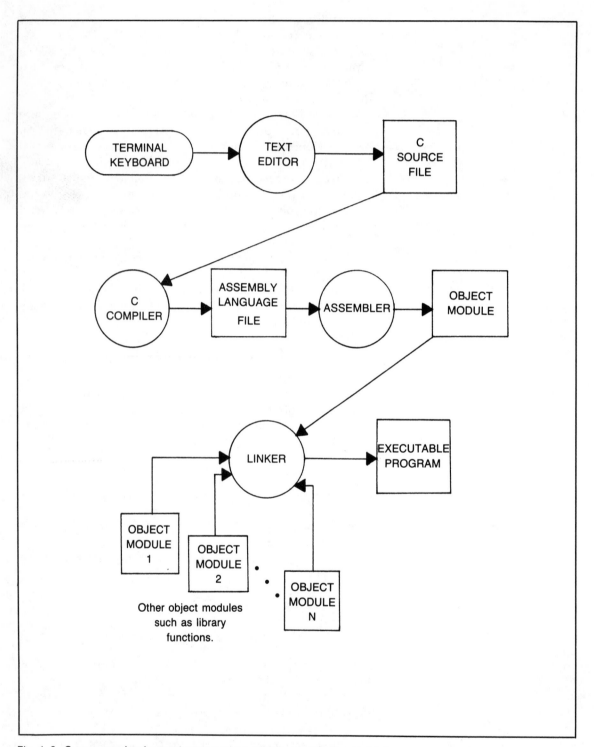

Fig. 1-2. C program development process: text editing, compilation and linkage.

Debugging

Because there are distinct phases of program development, some descriptive names have been invented to refer to them. The term *compile time* refers to the phase of compiling a source program into an object module. During compile time, the C compiler is performing the compilation. The term *link time* refers to the phase of development when separately compiled functions are being linked together. During link time, your system's linker is executing. Finally, there is *run time*. This is when you see the fruits of your labor. At run time, it is your program that is running.

When you are debugging a C program error messages will be reported at each phase. At compile time the C compiler reports syntax errors, for example, you left out a semicolon, or you misspelled a statement name. At link time the linker reports linkage errors, for example, a function you've used could not be found in the library. Finally, at run time you must find your logic errors. By testing the program, you will discover if it does what you intended it to do.

THE C PREPROCESSOR

You are now aware of the process required to create an executable C program, the process of compiling the source file and linking the object modules. The compilation process itself can be subdivided into two steps: a preprocessing step and a compilation step. The C preprocessor is a useful and often-used feature of the language. Because most of the example programs in this book use the preprocessor, we'll discuss some of its features now.

Consider a case in which specific numeric values are required in a program. For instance, assume that the numbers 3.141593 (an approximation of the number π) and 35700 (the maximum earnings subject to FICA taxes in 1983) are used. Embedding such numbers into a program can cause long term headaches. After leaving the program for a while, you can find yourself asking "what did 35700 mean, anyway?" Or, when the number is changed (and eventually the IRS will change 35700) you must search through the program to find every occurrence of the number, change them, and hope you caught them all.

The C preprocessor lets such numbers be defined symbolically. That is, you can define a symbol (or *token*) to represent the number, and then use the token throughout the program. Because the token is defined only once, its value can be changed throughout a program by changing only one statement. Further, if the token has a suggestive name (like PI, or

MAXFICA, for our examples) your program is more readable and easier to maintain.

Symbolic constants are defined by using the preprocessor statement *#define*. Unlike regular C statements, preprocessor statements are required to begin in column 1 of the source line. To define PI and MAXFICA as tokens, the following statements are used:

```
#define PI       3.141593
#define MAXFICA        35700
```

The preprocessor performs a token replacement on the source file. That is, wherever the token PI is used in the source file containing these #define statements, the token PI is replaced by the characters 3.141593. It is similar to the global search and replace action of a text editor, but different in that occurrences of the symbol PI embedded in other text are not replaced by the preprocessor. For example, if the token PICA also occurs in the program, the initial two characters of PICA are not replaced by the preprocessor. It is conventional to write such symbolic constants using all uppercase letters. That convention is followed in this text.

Basically, the preprocessor #define statement causes certain text in the source file to be replaced by other text. The simplest syntax of writing a #define statement is:

```
#define token_name   replacement_text
```

Syntactically, #define starts in column 1; one or more spaces (or tabs) separate it from the token name; then one or more spaces (or tabs) separate the token name from the replacement text. The replacement text is normally the rest of the line. If it is too long to fit on the line, a backslash character (\ ) is put at the end of the line and the replacement text can spill over to the next line. Also, a comment can appear at the end of the line, as in:

```
#define MAXFICA 35700  /*valid for 1983*/
```

The comment is not part of the replacement text, but just a comment. Once a token is defined in this way, its definition remains valid for the rest of the file. When replacing tokens, the preprocessor takes note of whether any of the replacement text is actually another token. Such tokens are also replaced by their replacement text. So, given the chain of #define statements:

```
/*Number of seconds per time unit*/

#define     MINUTE      60
#define     HOUR        60 * MINUTE
#define     DAY         24 * HOUR
#define     WEEK         7 * DAY
```

the token **WEEK** would be replaced in the program by the text:

```
7 * 24 * 60 * 60
```

When a token has been defined in a source file, the preprocessor leaves it unaltered when it occurs within quotation marks or within a comment. If MAXFICA has been defined as a token, then in:

```
printf("MAXFICA is 35700\n");
```

the string of characters "MAXFICA" would not be replaced by the preprocessor because they occur within quotation marks.

Another often-used feature of the preprocessor is the #include statement. Its syntax is:

```
#include "filename"
```

Like all preprocessor statements, it begins in column 1 of the source line. The #include statement reads the named file into the program. This file's text is inserted into the program at the point occupied by the #include statement. The double quotation marks serve to delimit the filename. Figure 1-3 illustrates the effect of the #include statement.

A variant of this statement is:

```
#include <filename>
```

When the filename is enclosed within angle brackets, it means that the file can be found in a prearranged place within the file system (a particular directory, for example). You will see an example of the use of the #include statement in the next section.

The C preprocessor provides other features that are discussed in Chapters 4 and 9. The result of adding the action of the C preprocessor to the C environment is depicted in Fig. 1-4. Figure 1-4 shows the flow of C program development from source statement entry via a text editor to the executable code produced by the system linker. The editor, preprocessor, compiler, and linker will be your fundamental tools in the C environment. Now that you know what the tools are and how

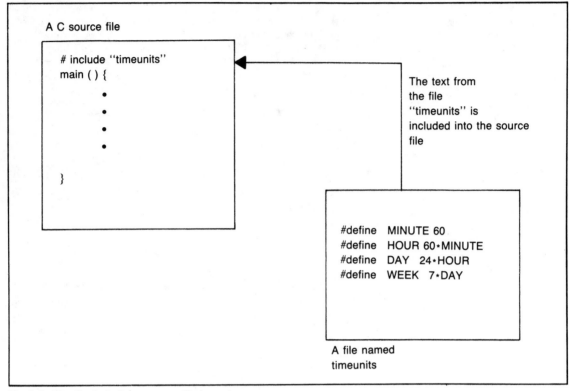

Fig. 1–3. The #include Preprocessor Statement.

they flow together, let's quickly examine how C programs write and read data to and from the outside world.

C INPUT AND OUTPUT

Input and output (I/O) operations are used to bring data into the program, and to enable the program to send information to the outside world. Typically, we think of I/O operations as being statements such as "read," "write," "input," and "print."

In the C language, there are no I/O statements. Rather, functions are used to perform I/O. C I/O functions are generally supplied by the manufacturer of a compiler. Because I/O is not formally specified by the language, there can be some variation in I/O from one compiler manufacturer to another. Fortunately, some standards have evolved. The I/O functions which are described in this book represent standard I/O functions as they are available in the marketplace. The standard I/O library was defined for UNIX systems. It has been adopted by most C compiler manufacturers; however, some C compilers provide nonstandard I/O.

10

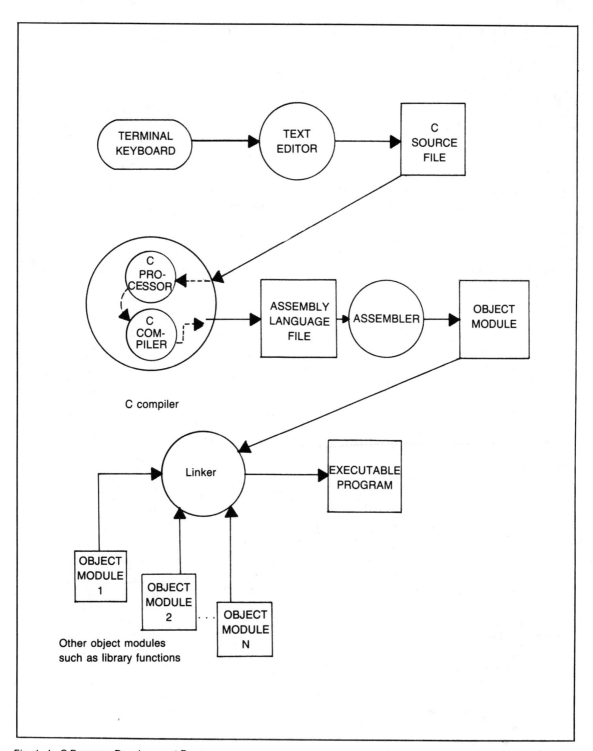

Fig. 1-4. C Program Development Process.

11

Common C I/O functions are *getchar*, *putchar*, and *printf*. Getchar is a standard input function. It reads one character from the "standard input stream" and returns that character to the program. The standard input stream is normally the keyboard of the terminal. We'll discuss the broader concept of standard input shortly.

In practice, the function getchar is used as:

```
c = getchar();
```

This use of getchar in a program causes the next character typed at the keyboard to be stored in the variable c. The parentheses after getchar indicate that getchar is a function. The parentheses are empty because the function is not being passed arguments.

Putchar is a standard output function that writes one character to the "standard output stream." The standard output stream is normally the terminal screen. The use of the function putchar in a program would appear like this:

```
putchar(c);
```

In this statement, c is a variable that presumably contains a character. The above statement writes the character to the terminal screen.

Because I/O is not formally a part of C, whenever these I/O functions are used in a program, it is necessary to include certain information that helps define the I/O operation in the program. This is done by the statement:

```
#include <stdio.h>
```

The file stdio.h contains declarations and preprocessor statements required by the I/O functions. The actual name of the file may be different from stdio.h; this varies for different compilers (see Exercise 1). In this book, the filename stdio.h is used. For your own programs, refer to the documentation supplied with your compiler.

As an example, the following program uses the I/O function putchar:

```
#include <stdio.h>

main() {
        putchar('w');
        putchar('e');
        putchar('l');
        putchar('c');
```

```
         putchar('o');
         putchar('m');
         putchar('e');

}
```

This program does exactly the same thing that our first program did. Here, the characters w,e,l,... are written to the standard output (the terminal screen) one character at a time. The single quotation marks around the letters indicate that the character is not a variable, but the actual character to be written.

The printf function also writes its output to the standard output stream. In general, printf performs "formatted" output. Its complete form is:

```
printf("format_info", argument-1, argument-2,...);
```

where arguments may or may not be present.

In the previous sections, we only used the "format_info" portion of printf. Characters in the format info portion are printed verbatim unless they're preceded by a backslash (\ ) or a percent sign (%). The backslash starts an escape sequence, and the percent sign begins a specification of how the arguments are to be printed. For example, in: *add new line*

```
printf( " %d is the current value of x\n ", x.);
```

the %d tells printf to format the first argument as a decimal integer. The first argument is the variable x. If the value of x is 13 at the time this statement is executed, then:

```
         13 is the current value of x
```

is printed. Further, when \n is included in the printf statement, the next printf (or putchar) statement will start printing on a new line. The various %-format specifiers are discussed in the next chapter.

In example programs in the next several chapters, getchar, putchar, and printf are used to perform I/O. Other I/O functions are introduced later.

⋆ STANDARD INPUT AND OUTPUT STREAMS

The notion of standard input and standard output is a feature of the UNIX environment that has followed C to other operating system environments as well. The concepts of standard input and standard output are easy to understand and they allow programs to be quite versatile in I/O.

13

Basically, standard input is "the place where the program's input comes from." By default, this is the keyboard of the terminal. So the statement:

```
c = getchar();
```

will read the next character typed at the keyboard and store that character in the variable c. The standard output is the "place where the program's output goes." This is normally the display of the terminal. Hence, the statement:

```
putchar(c);
```

writes whatever character is stored in the variable c to the terminal display.

The feature that makes standard I/O versatile in C environments is the capability to "redirect" the standard input and output at the time the program is run. For example, consider the following program, which reads one character from the standard input, then writes it to the standard output. <u>It is necessary to declare a variable to hold the character,</u> so the statement "int c;" is used:

```
#include <stdio.h>

main() {
    int c;   /* A variable declaration */

    c = getchar();
    putchar(c);
}
```

After compilation and linkage, assume that the name of the executable version of this program is "prog." Then the command to run the program is:

```
prog
```

When this command is issued, the program reads a character from the keyboard, writes the character to the screen, and exits. (When you run this program on your system, you may need to type a carriage return after typing a character.)

Alternatively, the command to run the program can be issued as:

```
prog <filex
```

from filex to screen

14

The notation "<filex" on the command line causes the redirection of the standard input. Now the standard input is a file named "filex." The one character that prog reads is the first character stored in filex. Because the standard output has not been redirected, it is still the terminal screen. Hence, when invoked in this way, the program reads one character from filex and writes that character to the terminal display.

The command line:

```
prog >filey
```

redirects the standard output. Now input is taken from the keyboard and output is sent to a file called filey. The command line:

```
prog <infile >outfile
```

redirects both the standard input and the standard output to the named files. Now prog reads one character from infile and writes it to outfile.

With redirection of standard I/O, the program does not have to be changed to use files for I/O instead of the keyboard and screen. The operating system takes care of the chores of opening and closing files or creating them when necessary. The capability to perform I/O redirection is not inherently a part of C, but it is a prevalent and useful feature of C programming environments. If you are still shopping for a C compiler, look for one that supports redirection of standard I/O.

A customary feature of the file stdio.h is the definition of a symbolic constant called EOF. When input is being read from a file, repeated calls to getchar will eventually reach the "end of the file." When this happens, getchar returns the value EOF. When getchar is reading the terminal keyboard, the user can signal that input is complete by typing a control code that means EOF. With UNIX, this is control d; with C/PM its control z. Whatever it is for your system, when it's typed, getchar will return EOF. By the way, it's never necessary to write an EOF when you've finished writing output to a file. The EOF is implicit at the end of the file.

There's nothing magic about EOF, it is just a token that means "end-of-file." Generally, it's defined as:

```
#define EOF -1
```

EOF = End of File

If the token EOF is not defined on your system, you can define it yourself. For instance, you can create a file called "mydefs," and put such things as:

```
#define EOF -1
#define TRUE 1
#define FALSE 0
#define SET TRUE
#define CLEAR FALSE
```

into the file. Then put the statement:

```
#include "mydefs"
```

near the beginning of your programs. You can then use all the tokens defined in "mydefs" in the program.

EXERCISES

1. Using your compiler's documentation:
   a. determine which of the following standard I/O library functions are available to you:

getchar	getc
putchar	putc
printf	scanf
getline	

   b. determine whether:

   ```
   #include <stdio.h>
   ```

   is the correct statement for using standard I/O functions with your compiler. If not, write the correct statement here:

   _____.

   Substitute this statement for #include <stdio.h> whenever you are using a program from this book.

2. Explain the difference between a "source program" and an "object program."

3. Using your text editor, write a C program to print your name and address. Compile, link, and execute the program.

4. If, in exercise 1a, you determined that getline is available to you:
   a. Enter the following program into your system:

```
#include <stdio.h>        /* If necessary, replace this
                             statement with the answer to
                             exercise 1b */

main() {

     char line[80];

     printf("Enter a line of text\n" );
     getline(line, 80);
     printf("The line you entered was:\n" );
     printf("%s", line);

}
```

define type of var
name of variable
number of characters allowed in variable array

means the following is a string or character variable

b. Compile, link, and execute the program. (Note: if the linker reports that getline is an unknown function, check your documentation on commands for linking programs to your I/O library.

c. Run the program. What does it do? *Allow input of one 80 character line & then displays it.*

5. Test whether your system supports redirection of the standard I/O by performing the following:

a. Enter the program that used putchar (page 12) into a file called test.c.

b. Compile and link test.c

c. Run the program using the command syntax:

(a.out >junk on UNIX systems)

d. Use a system utility such as dir on CP/M or MS-DOS, or ls under UNIX to see if a file called "junk" was created. What's in the file "junk"?

17

Chapter 2

Variables, Types, and Constants

There are basic parts of every programming language, and of course C is no exception. In this chapter, you will examine some of the basics of C—specifically, variables, types, and constants. We will define and provide examples of the basic C data types, illustrate how constants are written for each of these types, and show how they can be printed using the printf function. The discussion of printf expands upon the material presented in Chapter 1. Additionally, arrays and character strings are introduced.

It should be noted that new terms will be used in this chapter. We'll speak of decimal, octal, and hexadecimal numbers; scientific notation; as well as bytes and bits. No explanation of these terms is provided; however, you can refer to Appendix A for an explanation of these and other frequently used terms.

VARIABLES NAMES AND DECLARATIONS

Variables are like buckets that hold data. These buckets are really locations in the computer's memory. Variables give you a convenient way to name memory locations with names that are meaningful to our human memories.

Variable names begin with a letter and can contain letters or digits. The underscore character (_) is considered a letter and is often used to make variable names more readable. Examples of legal variable names are:

```
x
last_item
y75
_bufpoint
```

Some examples of illegal variable names are:

```
y$value
last#
7th_item
if
```

These names are illegal because the symbols $ and # cannot be used in variable names. The name "7th_item" starts with a digit, and "if" is a C keyword. A list of C keywords is shown in Table 2-1.

C keywords are words used as part of instructions or declarations. They are reserved and cannot be used as variable

Table 2-1 The C Keywords*.

The C keywords are shown below grouped according to use. Note that C keywords are always written in lowercase.

Integral Data Types:

char	int
short	long
unsigned	

Floating Point Data Types:

float	double

Other Data Types:

struct	union
typedef	enum

Storage Class Specifiers:

auto	extern
register	static

Statement Keywords:

if	switch
continue	case
else	default
for	entry
do	break
while	return
goto	void

Operator:

sizeof

*Notes:
1. The entry keyword has not been implemented by any C compiler.
2. Many C compilers do not use all of the above keywords.

names; however, they can be embedded in variable names, as in: int_flag, if_ready, and pchar.

In variable names upper- and lowercase letters are considered to be different. That is, the variable x is different from the variable X. Likewise, **counter** is different from **Counter**, and each is different from **COUNTER**. C programmers usually write variable names using lowercase letters. This book follows that convention.

symbolic constants = Capital
symbolic variables = lower case

Variable names can be as long as you like. Many compilers do not consider all of the characters as significant. For example, suppose that your compiler's documentation states that only eight characters of a variable name are significant. This means that a variable called "payroll_amt" is considered the same as one called "payroll_number" because their first eight characters are the same. However, you are free to use the longer variable names in your program.

All variables must be declared prior to use. Before you use a variable, you must tell the compiler its name and its type. There are different types of variables to hold different types of data. A variable's type tells the compiler what kind of data the variable will hold (an integer, for example). The declaration allows the compiler to set aside the correct amount of memory and proper memory alignment for the variable, and to generate appropriate code for its uses. The basic syntax of a variable declaration is:

```
Type Name Semicolon
```

For instance, the declarations:

```
int i;
char alpha;
```

declare the variables named i and alpha to be of type integer and character, respectively. According to the rules above, i and alpha are legal variable names.

More than one variable of a particular type can be declared on the same line by separating the variable names with a comma. For example:

```
int i,j,counter;
char alpha, c, beta;
```

declares three integer variables (i, j, and counter), and three character variables (alpha, c, and beta).

When declaring a variable, an initial value can be given to it by following its name with an equal sign, and the value, as in:

```
int j = 0;

int max = 1000;
```

These declarations define j and max as integer variables. Further, j is given the value 0, and max is given the value 1000. Not all compilers will perform initialization. You should check the specifications of your particular compiler to see if these declarations are legal.

INTEGER VARIABLES

Integers are the set of numbers:

```
MIN,....,-3,-2,-1,0,1,2,3,....,MAX
```

The largest integer (MAX) capable of being stored depends upon the machine you are using, and the way your compiler is implemented. The smallest integer (MIN) is similarly implementation dependent.

The C keyword *int* is used to declare integer variables. Int is used in declarations as:

```
int counter;
int j;
```

Typically, an int variable will hold numbers in the range of -32,768 to 32,767. This range may vary from machine to machine. The stated range implies that 16 bits are used to store an integer.

Suppose you want to use an integer variable, but you expect its value will be much larger than 32,767. C provides the adjective "long" for this instance. The declaration:

```
long int i;
```

serves to increase the capacity of i. A long int will typically hold numbers in the approximate range -2 billion to 2 billion.

When declaring a long int, it is acceptable to omit the word int. So, for example, the declarations:

```
long int galaxy, distance;
```

and

```
long galaxy,distance;
```

are synonymous. They each declare two long integer variables called galaxy and distance..

long int = long
int is optional
when used with a
qualifier

At the other end of the size spectrum is the adjective "short." If it is known that an integer variable will remain relatively small, you can declare:

```
short int j;
short small_count, length;
```

As with "long," the word "int" can be omitted when declaring a short int.

It should be noted that the capacity of both long and short integer variables is machine dependent. You need to examine your compiler's documentation to determine the size of these objects on your system.

Finally, there is one last applicable adjective—"unsigned." For situations where it is known that an integer will never be negative, you can declare it as unsigned. For example:

```
unsigned int absval;
```

or

```
unsigned address1,address2;
```

Typically, an unsigned int will have a range of 0 to 65,535. Again, int can be omitted. Unsigned is a natural type for quantities in a program that are, by nature, unsigned. An example of such a quantity might be an address within memory.

The range of numbers that can be stored in int, short, long, and unsigned variables is not guaranteed by C itself. The ranges stated above are typical of eight- and 16-bit systems. What C does guarantee is that "short" will be no longer than "int;" "long" will be at least as long as "int;" and "unsigned" will never be negative. Beyond this, check the specifications of the compiler you are using.

INTEGER CONSTANTS

Constants are the data items in a program that remain the same throughout the program. In C, integer constants can be expressed in a variety of ways. You can express integer constants in decimal, octal, or hexadecimal notation. (See Appendix A if you are not familiar with these numbering systems). Further, you can explicitly state that a constant is long.

Decimal (base 10) integers are written as: 783, 5, 27961, 0, or -338. Writing 27961 illustrates that commas are not used in constants. For example, writing 27,961 is not correct.

Octal (base 8) constants are written with a leading zero: 052, 0131, or 012. These octal constants have decimal values of 42, 89, and 10, respectively.

No commas are used as place holders

Hexadecimal constants (base 16) are indicated by a preceding 0x or 0X (zero x). The digits 0–9 and the letters a–f (or A–F) are used to represent hexadecimal digit. For example Ox2f (or OX2F) and Ox9a (or OX9A) are hexadecimal constants.

Long int constants are indicated by a trailing "L." Therefore 4978L and 32567821L are two long decimal constants. Though a lowercase l is legal, we're using the uppercase L because the lowercase looks so much like a number one. Also, if an integer constant is written which is too big for int, the compiler will store it as a long. For example, the integer constant 33582 would be stored as a long if 32767 is the largest int your compiler will represent.

In a similar fashion, long octal constants and long hexadecimal constants can be written:

```
0735L    /*a long octal constant*/
OX5AA8L  /* a long hexadecimal constant*/
OXBEEFL  /* another long hex constant*/
```

The preceding zero of the first example indicates that 0735L is a long octal constant. The preceding OX of the second example indicates that is a long hexadecimal constant.

PRINTING INTEGERS WITH PRINTF

Printf can be used to print the value of integer variables. In Chapter 1, the general form of printf was introduced as:

```
printf("format_info", argument-1, argument-2,...)
```

To print integers with printf, the following conversion specifications can be used:

```
%c  /* print the ASCII symbol for the number stored in the variable*/
%d  /* print the integer in decimal notation */

%o  /* print the integer in octal octal notation */

%x  /* print in integer in hexadecimal notation */
%f  /* print number with a decimal point eg - floating point*/
%e  /* print number in scientific notation form */
```

For example, to print an integer variable named "counter" in decimal format, the statement

```
printf("%d",counter);
```

is used. This statement prints the value of counter on the standard output.

format

The number of conversion specifications used in a printf statement must match the number of arguments to be printed. For instance:

```
printf("%d %o %x", counter, address, value);
```

prints counter in decimal notation, address in octal notation, and value in hexadecimal notation. Because three conversion specifications are given, three variable names are present. If the number of format specifiers is different from the number of variables, an error will result. In the last example, the spaces between the conversion specifiers will result in printed spaces between the numbers. When written as:

```
printf("%d%o%x", counter, address, value);
```

no extra space will be printed between the numbers. When written as:

```
printf("%d\n%o\n%x\n", counter, address, value);
```

each number is printed on a different line.

Program Listing 2-1 and its output (Fig. 2-1) illustrate the appearance of integers printed by printf.

```
       The %d Format
       :1:14:
       :8976:14:
       :8976:32289:


       The %o Format
       :1:16:
       :21420:16:
       :21420:77041:


       The %x Format
       :1:E:
       :2310:E:
       :2310:7E21:
```

Fig. 2-1. Sample program output from printing integers with printf. Output may appear different on your system.

Listing 2-1. Illustration of integers printed by Printf.

```
#include <stdio.h>

main() { /* Test how printf prints integers */

        int x = 1;
        int y = 8976;
        int z = 32289;
        int i = 14;

        /*  Test the %d Format  */
        printf("The %%d Format\n");
        printf(":%d:%d:", x,i);
        printf("\n");

        printf(":%d:%d:",y,i);
        printf("\n");

        printf(":%d:%d:",y,z);
        printf("\n\n\n");

        /*  Test the %o Format  */
        printf("The %%o Format\n");
        printf(":%o:%o:", x,i);
        printf("\n");

        printf(":%o:%o:",y,i);
        printf("\n");

        printf(":%o:%o:",y,z);
        printf("\n\n\n");

        /*  Test the %x Format  */
        printf("The %%x Format\n");
        printf(":%x:%x:", x,i);
        printf("\n");

        printf(":%x:%x:",y,i);
        printf("\n");

        printf(":%x:%x:",y,z);
        printf("\n");
}
```

The colons used in the printf statements are just ordinary characters printed verbatim. They help to show how spaces are printed between the numbers. Examine the program and the figure to see how the % character was printed. Since the % character has a special meaning within the format portion of printf, you need to use %% when you actually want the % character to be printed.

Try running this program on your system to test how your printf function prints integers. The spacing of integers may differ on your system as printf's printing format depends on the compiler you are using. You can gain much finer control over how an integer will be printed; this will be discussed in Chapter 8.

[handwritten: → & therefore must have an "L" at the end of it.]

Finally, if the integer to be printed is a long int, the letter l is used just before the conversion character. For instance:

[handwritten: Format character %d]

```
long bignum = 19803215L;

printf("%ld", bignum);
```

print the value of the long integer bignum in decimal notation. The statements:

```
printf("%lx", bignum);
printf("%lo", bignum);
```

print it in hexadecimal then octal notation.

FLOAT AND DOUBLE VARIABLES AND CONSTANTS

Float and *double* are the C data types used to represent rational numbers. Rational numbers have a whole part and a fractional part, such as: 4.621, 143.0, -7.5865329, or 0.00007. These numbers are generally called *floating point numbers*; hence, the name of the C data type—"float." The *precision* of a floating point number relates to the number of significant digits that can be represented in storage. For example, 3.14 is an approximation of the number π, but 3.14159 is a more *precise* approximation as it contains more significant digits.

A double-precision number is capable of storing more significant digits than a single-precision number. Double is the name of the C double-precision floating-point data type.

The following statements illustrate how float and double variables are declared:

```
float radius, circum;

double arclen, result;
```

Double does not imply that a variable so typed can hold twice the precision of float. Indeed, double usually holds more than twice the precision. The exact specifications are, again, complier dependent.

It is acceptable to use the adjective long with float, as in:

```
long float arclen, result;
```

This has the same meaning as double.

Floating point constants are written as: 37.51, 1298.6, or 10.0. The fractional portion of the floating point constant is to the right of the decimal point. No spaces are allowed within the number. Scientific notation (see Appendix A) can also be used, as in: 3.21e4, 7.65E-5, or 0.11e2, which mean 3.21×10^4, 7.65×10^{-5}, and 0.11×10^2, respectively. All floating point constants are stored with the precision of double, so they serve both the float and double data types.

PRINTING FLOATS AND DOUBLES WITH PRINTF

If x is a float or double variable, its value can be printed with printf using the %f conversion specification. An example is:

Format

```
printf("%f", x);
```

The %f conversion specification prints the number with a decimal point.

Alternatively, floats and doubles can be printed using the %e conversion specification. With a %e specification, printf prints the number in scientific notation.

Program Listing 2-2 and its output (Fig. 2-2) illustrate how floats and doubles are printed by printf. As with printing integers, you can gain additional control over how a float or double is printed; the details of gaining this additional control are presented in Chapter 8.

```
The %f Format
:3.210000:-21.533400:2.578000:-.000040:


The %e Format
:3.210000E0:-2.153340E1:2.578000E0:-4.000000E-5:
```

Fig. 2-2. Program output from printing floating point values with printf. Output may appear different on your system.

Listing 2–2. Illustration of floats and doubles printed by Printf.

```
#include <stdio.h>

main() {

        float r = 3.21, t = -2.15334e1;
        double x = 2.578, y = -0.4e-4;

        printf("The %%f Format\n");
        printf(":%f:%f:%f:%f: \n\n\n", r,t,x,y);


        printf("The %%e Format\n");
        printf(":%e:%e:%e:%e: \n\n\n", r,t,x,y);

}
```

CHARACTER VARIABLES AND CONSTANTS

Character variables are declared in the following way:

```
char alpha, beta, c;
```

This declaration declares the variables alpha, beta, and c to be of type character.

A character variable can store one byte of information. Although you tend to think of characters as letters of the alphabet (a,b,...A,B...), punctuation symbols (!;,?), and so on, internally the computer stores characters as zeros and ones. These zeros and ones are interpreted as a code to determine which character is being represented.

On many machines (particularly mini- and microcomputers) the American Standard Code for Information Interchange (ASCII) is used. The ASCII code associates a unique character with the numeric values between 0–128 (decimal). Hence, ASCII associates a character with every possible seven-bit combination of zeros and ones. (The eighth bit is called the parity bit. It is used for error detection, and is not discussed further in this text.)

In Table 2–2, the letters and digits are shown cross-referenced to their values according to the ASCII code. (In Appendix B, a table of all ASCII characters is presented.) Table 2–2 indicates, for example, that the bit pattern used to store the letter A has a decimal value of 65. The decimal value of the character 9 is 57 in ASCII. That may sound a bit confusing, but more examples follow to help clarify this situation.

A character constant is written in C by enclosing the character in single quotation marks. The following declara-

IBM uses
EBIDC
Binary Coded Decimal

28

Table 2-2 Numeric Values of ASCII Letters and Digits.

| Char | Numeric Values | | | Char | Numeric Values | | |
	dec	oct	hex		dec	oct	hex
0	48	60	30	5	53	65	35
1	49	61	31	6	54	66	36
2	50	62	32	7	55	67	37
3	51	63	33	8	56	70	38
4	52	64	34	9	57	71	39
A	65	101	41	a	97	141	61
B	66	102	42	b	98	142	62
C	67	103	43	c	99	143	63
D	68	104	44	d	100	144	64
E	69	105	45	e	101	145	65
F	70	106	46	f	102	146	66
G	71	107	47	g	103	147	67
H	72	110	48	h	104	150	68
I	73	111	49	i	105	151	69
J	74	112	4A	j	106	152	6A
K	75	113	4B	k	107	153	6B
L	76	114	4C	l	108	154	6C
M	77	115	4D	m	109	155	6D
N	78	116	4E	n	110	156	6E
O	79	117	4F	o	111	157	6F
P	80	120	50	p	112	160	70
Q	81	121	51	q	113	161	71
R	82	122	52	r	114	162	72
S	83	123	53	s	115	163	73
T	84	124	54	t	116	164	74
U	85	125	55	u	117	165	75
V	86	126	56	v	118	166	76
W	87	127	57	w	119	167	77
X	88	130	58	x	120	170	78
Y	89	131	59	y	121	171	79
Z	90	132	5A	z	122	172	7A

tions illustrate the use of character constants as variable initializers:

```
char alpha = 'a';
char beta = 'b';
char capb = 'B';
char plus = '+';
char dolsign = '$';
```

Alpha is declared to be a character variable and is initialized to hold the character constant 'a'. Similarly, beta is initialized to 'b', capb to 'B', etc.

There are some characters that are difficult or even impossible to see. For example, the character constant for "space" appears as follows:

```
char space = ' ';
```

This works properly in a program if the space bar is depressed between the two single quotation marks.

If you try the same method of specifying the character constant "backspace," that declaration would probably get printed like this:

```
char backspace = ';  /* wrong way to initialize backspace*/
```

Typing the key sequence "single quote, backspace, single quote" will likely get backspaced on itself while printing and is thus hard to read.

To bring these hidden characters into the open, C provides *escape sequences*. Character escape sequences start with a backslash (\) and are show in Table 2-3. The \n escape sequence has been used repeatedly in printf statements.

Character escape sequences can be used between single quotation marks to represent the specified character. For example:

```
char backspace = '\b';
char tab = '\t';
char single_quote = '\'';
char backslash = '\\';
char newline = '\n';
```

declares the variable "backspace" and initializes it to the backspace character. Similarly, "tab" is declared and initialized to the tab character. Since the single quotation mark is used to delimit the escape sequence, it is necessary to use the escape sequence \' to represent the single quotation mark itself. Similarly, the backslash character itself is represented by the escape sequence \\. Even though escape sequences appear as two characters, they will be represented as one character in the computer.

Table 2-3 Common C Character Escape Sequences.

Escape Sequence	Meaning	ASCII Symbol
\b	backspace	BS
\f	form feed	FF
\n	new line	LF
\r	carriage return	CR
\t	horizontal tab	HT
\\	backslash	\
\'	single quote	'
\0	octal value 0	NUL
\xxx	octal value xxx	(arbitrary value xxx)

used for bit pattern masks

The last escape sequence of Table 2-3, \xxx, allows the programmer to define a character constant by stating the value of the desired character in octal. For instance:

```
char c = '\071';
```

initializes c to the octal value 071. In ASCII, this value represents the character '9' (refer to Table 2-2) The same result is better obtained by the statement:

```
char c = '9';
```

The xxx can be one, two, or three octal digits. The escape sequence \xxx is most often used to store specific bit patterns in variables. This is discussed in Chapter 9.

The escape sequences can also be used in preprocessor statements. For example:

```
                                  ascⅡ Tab number
#define TAB '\t'
#define CARRIAGE_RETURN '\r'        ascⅡ CR number
#define NULL '\0'    000 octal = ASCⅡ Null
```

It is important to understand the difference between the initialization:

```
char alpha = '0'; and
```

and

```
char alpha = '\0';
```

The first initializes alpha to the character zero which in ASCII has a value of 48 (060 in octal). The second initializes alpha to the value of zero, which in ASCII is called the null character.

PRINTING CHARACTERS WITH PRINTF

To print a character with printf, a %c conversion specification is used. As an example, the program:

```
#include <stdio.h>

main() {

    char c = 'H';
    char d = 'I';
    char e = '!';
```

```
        printf("%c%c%c", c, d, e);
    }
```

prints: HI!

CHARACTER STRINGS *— don't exist in C — they are listed as an array of individual variables.*

When single characters are placed one after the other, the result is called a character string. Character strings are written as contiguous characters enclosed in double quotation marks (''). For example: ''This is a string'' is a string constant or string literal. Strings are stored in memory as follows:

| T | h | i | s | | i | s | | a | | s | t | r | i | n | g | \0 |

The double quotation marks at each end of the string literal are delimiters. They are not part of the string, but serve to mark the beginning and the end. When the string literal is stored, the C compiler automatically terminates it with a null character (\0). The null character serves as an in memory end-of-string marker. In this example, ''This is a string'' uses 17 bytes of storage—16 for letters and spaces, and one for the end-of-string marker.

Take note of the fact that a character constant such as 'a' is different from the string constant ''a''; 'a' is a single character, while ''a'' is a string consisting of the character 'a' and the end-of-string marker '\0'. The string '''' is valid.. It is an empty string containing the end-of-string marker only.

Unlike such languages as BASIC, C does not have a string variable type. Instead, arrays of characters are used. Since a string uses contiguous character locations, an array is a natural way to represent them. With this in mind, let's examine the basics of arrays.

ARRAY BASICS

Conceptually, an array is a sequence of related variables. These variables are related by the fact that they all have the same name and type and are stored contiguously in memory. Each variable is called an element of the array. For instance, the declaration:

```
char string[4];
```

declares string to be an array with four elements. The square brackets after the name are used to indicate that an array is being declared. The 4 within the brackets specifies how many elements the array has. Thus, four character variables (string[0], string[1], string[2], and string[3]) are defined. The individual variables are accessed by the array name and an index value. In the term "string[0]", the 0 is the index of the first array element. Note that C begins the indexing of array elements with zero.

It is valid to define an array of any C data type that has been discussed so far. For example:

```
int number[100];        /*an int array*/
float values[10], x[35]; /*two float arrays*/
double y[50];           /*a double array*/
```

The first of these declarations defines 100 integer variables called number[0], number[1], ..., number[99].

An integer variable can be used as an array index. For example:

```
int i,j;
i = 30;
j = number[i];    @Defines j as a variable array
                     with the size 30
```

places the value of number[30] into the variable j. Floating point variables cannot be used as array indices, even if they hold integer values. For example:

```
int j;
float f;
f = 30;
j = number[f];   /*WRONG*/
```

When declaring arrays, it is quite natural to use the C preprocessor to define the size of the array as a symbolic constant. For example:

```
#define NAMESIZE 20       Let Namesize = 20
#define BUFSIZE 512        Let Bufsize = 512

char name[NAMESIZE];    initialize variable name = 20
char buffer[BUFSIZE];        "      "    buffer = 512
```

The use of the #define statement in this application will let you adjust the size of arrays in your program without having to search through the program to find the actual array declarations.

The concept of a character string constant was introduced in the last section. Now you can put it into the context of the character array. The declaration:

```
char s[17] = "This is a string";
```

the array must always be one Larger than the string to allow for the null terminator at the end.

33

performs an initialization of the character array "s", and leaves:

```
s[0] containing T
s[1] containing h
s[2] containing i
       .
       .
       .
s[15] containing g
s[16] containing '\0'
```

Notice that 17 is the size of the array s. We made s big enough to hold the characters and the end-of-string marker. Fig. 2–3 illustrates the contiguous nature of storage provided for the arrays.

When strings are used to initialize character arrays, counting the number of characters and sizing the array accordingly is

Memory Contents	Array Element
T	string[0]
h	string[1]
i	string[2]
s	string[3]
	string[4]
i	string[5]
s	string[6]
	string[7]
a	string[8]
	string[9]
s	string[10]
t	string[11]
r	string[12]
i	string[13]
n	string[14]
g	string[15]
/0	string[16]

Fig. 2–3. Storage of char array defined by: char[ ] = "This is a string";.

quite tedious. Fortunately, C eliminates this tedium. The declaration:

```
char s[] = "This is a string";
```

performs the same initialization as the one above. Since the array s is being initialized, it is not necessary to include the size of the array in the declaration. The compiler will count the number of initializers present, add one for the end-of-string marker, and size the array accordingly. There are some restrictions on when an array can be initialized. We'll discuss the restrictions in Chapter 3.

The escape sequences used inside the single quotation marks for character constants can also be used inside the double quotation marks of string constants. For example:

```
"This is a string\n"
```

has a newline character at the end of the text. The string:

```
"Salesman\t\tSales\tCommissions\n\n"
```

separates the words "Salesman" and "Sales" with two tab characters; separates "Sales" and "Commissions" with one tab character; and puts two new line characters at the end of the string. Each of these strings is terminated with the null character.

The program:

```
#include <stdio.h>

main() { /*Sales Summary Report*/

    printf("\t\tSALES SUMMARY\n\n");
    printf("NAME\t\tSALES\tCOMMISSIONS\n\n");
    printf("JOHN\t\t2000\t375\n");
    printf("MARY\t\t1590\t210\n");
    printf("BILL\t\t1250\t180\n");
}
```

prints a report as:

```
          SALES SUMMARY
NAME             SALES          COMMISSIONS

JOHN             2000           375
MARY             1590           210
BILL             1250           180
```

To embed a double quotation mark inside a string, the backslash escape is used. For instance, the program:

the backslash tells C to convert the following characters to ASCII & not to try to interpret its symbolic meaning in C if it has any.

```
main() {

printf("two \"quotes\" in this string.");

}
```

prints: two "quotes" in this string.

PRINTING CHARACTER ARRAYS WITH PRINTF

When a character array contains a string of characters, the string can be printed using the %s conversion specification. The following example illustrates this:

```
#include <stdio.h>

char string1[] = "Stings are printed";
char string2[] = " with the %s conversion specification."

main() {

    printf("%s", string1);
    printf("%s\n", string2);
}
```

Note that only the array name is given in the printf statement. For instance, writing:

```
    printf("%s", string1[0]);   /* WRONG */
```

is not correct. Further, strings must be terminated with the end-of-string marker to be correctly printed. The printf function uses the end-of-string marker to determine when printing is complete. If the marker is not present, erroneous characters will be printed.

As a simple example of printing character arrays, the program:

```
    #include <stdio.h>

    char mother[] = "MOM";
    char father[] = "DAD";
```

```
main() {

    printf("Hello %s !\n", mother);
    printf("Hello %s !\n", father);

}
```

[handwritten annotation: %s means print the following variable as a string array whose length was]

[handwritten annotation: → automatically calculated the size using the ~~X[]~~ char X[] = "xxx"]

prints:

Hello MOM !
Hello DAD !

EXERCISES

1. Which of the following are illegal C variable names? Why?
   - a. x31
   - b. 5times
   - c. allabout
   - d. NEXT_item
   - e. ___buf_
   - f. $xval
   - g. save!
   - h. break
   - i. time_to_rexecute_loop21
   - j. A

2. Which of the following are illegal decimal constants? Why?
   - a. 2,783 *[handwritten: commas not allowed]*
   - b. -1
   - c. 785
   - d. $21.00
   - e. 0361 *[handwritten: ← octal constant leading 0]*
   - f. 4.25

3. Which of the following are illegal octal constants? Why?
   - a. 021
   - b. 0784
   - c. 0
   - d. 1235
   - e. 0x03
   - f. 006

4. Which of the following are illegal hexadecimal constants? Why?
   - a. 0XAB
   - b. 0x321F
   - c. x35B
   - d. 0X15G4
   - e. 0X21.7
   - f. FFFF

5. What will the following program print?

```
#include <stdio.h>

char text[] = "Printing Example";

main() {

    printf("%s\n", text);
    printf("%c%c\n%c\n", text[0], text[1], text[2]);

}
```

6. Which of the following are invalid string literals? Why?
   - a. "Hello"
   - b. "Hello\n"
   - c. "Hello"World"
   - d. "178921"
   - e. "A\"must\"issue"
   - f. 'short cut'
   - g. "The end. $"
   - h. ".,:!"

7. Three lines in the following program contain errors. Find and explain the errors.

```
#include <stdio.h>

int i = 15;
int m = 21

int number[15];
int j;

main () {

        number[0] = i;
        printf("%n", i);
        j = number(0);
        printf("%d",j);


}
```

Try compiling this program as is on your system. What errors does your compiler report?

Chapter 3

Overview of a C Program

Before diving into the depths of statement writing, this chapter pauses for a moment to examine an overview of a C program. In the last chapter you learned how to declare and initialize various types of variables. You have also seen a few C functions—main, getchar, putchar, printf, etc. In this chapter you will take a more detailed look at how data objects (variables and constants) and computation objects (functions) come together to form a C program.

FUNCTIONS

Previously we described a function as a "black box of logic and computation." The notion of a black box implies that the function does a particular job. The user of the function need not be concerned about how the job is done, only that it is done.

For instance, most computer terminals will let the screen be cleared and the cursor be positioned at a particular row and column. To make these things happen under program control, the program must send certain characters to the screen. For example, with the Digital Equipment Corporation VT52 terminal the cursor can be positioned at row 1 column 1 by sending the terminal an ASCII ESC character followed by the character 'H'. You can easily write a function to do this:

```
#define ESC '\033'   /*the ASCII escape*/

home_cursor() { /*Home cursor on VT52 terminal*/

       putchar(ESC);
       putchar('H');

}
```

Now that this function is in place, it can be called by other functions.

On the same VT52 terminal, the characters ESC and 'J' cause the data on the screen to be erased from the current cursor position to the end of the screen. Using this information (and home_cursor) you can write the function clear_screen:

```
clear_screen() {

       /*clear VT52 terminal screen*/

       home_curs();
       putchar(ESC);
       putchar('J');

}
```

Clear_screen is a black box that performs the function of clearing the terminal's display. If you wish to clear the screen in your program you can call clear_screen to do it for you. You no longer need be concerned with how it is done, only that clear_screen will do it.

In C, to call a function you simply write its name. In the function clear_screen, the line:

```
home_curs();
```

calls the function home_curs to reposition the cursor. For a program to call_clear screen, the following statement would be used:

```
clear_screen();
```

Suppose that you want to write a function called "set_cursor" to position the display's cursor. This function will need a bit more information than clear_screen did. You will have to tell set cursor at which row and column to position the cursor. You can envision making a call to the function like:

```
set_cursor(5,10);
```

40

meaning "place the cursor at row 5, column 10." In this call to the function, 5 and 10 are called *arguments*. The arguments are passed to the function when it is called.

Assume that the terminal you are using has 24 rows and 80 columns. What should set cursor do if you call it with arguments:

```
set_cursor(37,102);
```

It would be nice if set cursor could indicate that an error has been detected. To do this, set cursor must return some information. C functions can return one value. For instance, set cursor might return different integer values as a signal meaning OK, or **ERROR**. To capture this returned information, a function calling set cursor would use a statement of the following form:

```
n = set_cursor(5,10);
```

This causes set cursor to perform its task. Further, the value returned by set cursor is stored in the variable n.

Our discussion leads you to a conceptual view of a C function. It is a black box that performs a particular task. When it is called by another function, information is passed to it through arguments. When necessary, it can return a result. In the following sections, we'll put a little more meat on these conceptual bones.

DEFINING FUNCTIONS

Before we discuss how to write functions, let's establish a bit of terminology. If function A calls function B, we'll say that function A is the *caller* (or the calling function), and that function B is the *called* function. For example, in the program:

```
#include <stdio.h>

main() {
    printf("welcome");

}
```

"main" is the caller, and "printf" is the called function.

Suppose the function main must call another function to perform a task. What will main need to know? Main will need to know the function's name; the number and type of arguments the function expects; and the type of result the function will return. This leads to the syntax for defining functions.

Functions are defined by the syntax:

```
return_type  func_name(arguments,if any)
    argument_declarations

{

    /*the function's declarations*/
                    .
                    .
                    .
    /*the function's executable statements*/
}
```

"Return_type" tells the type of result the function will return (e.g., int, char, float, double, etc.). If the return type is not specified, the compiler assumes the function returns an int.

"Func_name" is the function's name. Function names follow the same rules as variable names—they start with a letter (an underscore is considered a letter), and are composed of letters and digits, etc. (see Chapter 2). A left parenthesis (( ) always follows the function name. Within the parentheses is a list of names, one name for each value to be passed to the function. The names are separated by commas. The right parenthesis ( )) closes this list. This list of names is called the parameter list. If the function is not passed data, then no names appear between the parentheses (you saw with clear_screen( )).

Next, declarations are made to specify the type represented by each name in the parameter list. For example:

```
float power(x,n)
    float x;
    int n;
```

begins the definition of a function called power. It returns a float to its caller. Its first argument will be a float, its second argument an int. If a name in the parameter list is not declared, the compiler will assume that it is an int. The left brace ({) then begins the function's variable declaration and executable statements.

Figure 3-1 shows several examples of the syntax. Notice in Fig. 3-1 that you are free to position the various parts of the function definition as you wish. For instance, in the "sqrt" function, the information spans several lines; in the "big" function, it's all on one line.

When a function returns an int (as big and heavy do) it is not necessary to specify the return type. So those functions could have been defined as:

```
heavy() {}
```

and

```
           int heavy ()
              {
              }
```

Heavy is a function
that returns in int.
It will not be passed
arguments.

```
        double
        sqrt(x,tolerance)

        double x;
        float tolerance;
        {
        }
```

Sqrt is a function that
will return a double.
It takes two arguments.
The first argument will
be a second type. The
second will be a float.

```
        char stringfix(s,j)
             char s;
             int j;
         {
         }
```

Stringfix is a function that
returns a char. It will receive two arguments.
The first will be a char, the second
int.

```
        int big(n) int n; {  }
```

Big is a function that will
return an int. It will be
passed one argument, an int.

Fig. 3-1. Examples of C function definitions.

```
big <n> int n; {}
```

In other words, when a return type is not specified, the compiler
assumes that the function will return an int. Such assumptions
by the compiler are usually called the *defaults.*

Even though there are no statements between the braces of
these functions, they are all legal C functions. You can actually
enter them into your system and compile them without error.
They are all do-nothing functions, or *null functions.*

Null functions can be useful. For example, suppose you are
writing a large program and you've divided it into several
functions, one of which is called "hard." Then during development, you can insert hard into your program like this:

43

```
hard() {

    /* write this function later*/

}
```

Should some other function in your developing program call hard, this temporary version will satisfy the compiler. The null version of hard will allow compiles and links to take place so that you can test other functions.

FUNCTIONS AND LOCAL VARIABLES

To make a function perform a task, statements are written between the function's braces. We'll explain this process now, using simple program statements.

Consider the following function called average:

```
average(amt1,amt2)
    int amt1,amt2;
{

    int answer;

    answer = amt1 + amt2;
    answer = answer/2;

    return (answer);

}
```

From the last section you know that average returns an integer value to its caller (the default return type), and that average is passed two arguments. The line: int amt1, amt2; specifies that the arguments are integers.

Now, look inside average's braces. First, an int variable called answer is declared. Since answer is declared inside the braces of the function, it belongs to the function exclusively. That is, no other function has access to this variable. In this sense, answer is a *local variable*. It is local to the function average. In C, it is called an *automatic variable*. Conceptually, it automatically comes into being when a function is called and automatically disappears when the function returns. The C keyword *auto* can be used to explicitly state that a variable is automatic. Hence, answer could be declared as:

```
auto int answer;
```

Since all variables declared inside of functions are auto by default, this is seldom done.

If another function (say, five) has a variable called answer:

```
five() (
        int answer;
        answer = 5
        return (answer);

)
```

the variable answer in average is totally different from the variable answer in five. They are each local to their respective functions.

In average, the statements:

$$answer = amt1 + amt2;$$
$$answer = answer/2;$$

perform the logic of average. They use three operators (+, =, and /), which will be discussed in the next chapter. Basically, the first statement adds (+) amt1 and amt2, then assigns (=) the sum to the variable answer. The second divides (/) that sum by 2 and puts the result of the division back into the variable answer. The third statement:

```
return(answer);
```

is the mechanism that allows average to pass information back to the calling function. In addition to returning a value, when a return statement is executed in a function the function terminates and its automatic variables disappear. The next statement to be executed will be in the function that called it.

The parenthesis after "return" may have fooled you. Return is not a function, but a statement. It is also correct to write:

```
return answer;
```

Further, when functions have no information to return you can simply write:

```
return;
```

For example, clear screen could have been written:

```
#define ESC    '\033'
clear_screen()   (
        home_curs();
        putchar(ESC);
```

```
        putchar('J');
        return;
    }
```

However, when a function has nothing to return, most C programmers leave the return statement out altogether. Functions always return when they reach their terminating brace. It's good to remember that return is not a function, because if you write:

```
clear_screen()  {
        home_curs();
        putchar(ESC);
        putchar('J');
        return();   /*WRONG*/
    }
```

the compiler will complain and refuse to compile your program. Figure 3-2 is a complete program that uses the function average.

```
        /* Preprocessor Statements */
#include <stdio.h>
#define   NAMESIZE 15

        /* Global Variables */
int count;
char name[NAMESIZE] = "John Doe";

        /* Function 1 */
initialize_count()
{
        count = 0;
}

        /* Function 2 */
bump_count()
{
        count = count + 1;
}

        /* Function main */
main()
{
        initialize_count();
        printf("%s\n", name);
        bump_count();
        printf("%s\n", name);
        bump_count();

        printf("The name %s was printed %d times\n", name, count);
}
```

Fig. 3-2. A program using the function "average."

46

GLOBAL VARIABLES

As you see, whenever a variable is declared inside a function it is local to the function. The phrase *scope of a variable name* is used in this context. The scope of a variable is the portion of the program over which its name is known. When a variable is local to a function, its scope is the function in which it is declared. When the function ends with the terminating brace, the local variable names are meaningless. *(Their values are cleared & names may be reused)*

When a variable is declared outside any function it is a *global variable*. A global variable can be accessed by all functions. For example, consider the following program:

```
#include <stdio.h>

int count;    /*a global variable*/

main()  (
      count = 10;
      bumpit();
      bumpit();
      bumpit();
      printf("%d", count);

)
bumpit()  (
      count = count + 1;
)
```

In this program, both functions—main and bumpit—have access to the variable count since it is defined outside these functions. Thus, main sets count to the value 10 and calls bumpit three times. On each call, bumpit adds one to count. Hence, this program prints:

13

Global variables are a second way that functions can share information. Remember that the first was by passing arguments and using the return statement.

If your programming background is in BASIC you are most familiar with global variables. In most versions of BASIC all variables are global. In C, only variables declared outside of functions are global.

Consider what you might think is another way to write the above program:

```
#include <stdio.h>

main()  (
```

```
        int count;   /*local to main*/

        count = 10;
        bumpit();
        bumpit();
        bumpit();

        printf("%d", count);

    }

bumpit() (
        int count;   /*local to bumpit*/
             count = count + 1;

    }
```

In this version, each function has a local variable called count. These are automatic variables. The count in main is not related to the count in bumpit. Hence, when main calls bumpit three times, this has no affect on main's count. Therefore, this program prints:

10

Once a global variable is declared in a source file, it can be used by any function subsequently defined in the same source file. For this reason, global variables are often declared near the beginning of the program.

Global variables are also accessible to functions defined in other source files, or to functions defined prior to the declaration of the global variable. However, in these cases an extra declaration is required. This will be discussed in Chapter 9.

FORMAL PARAMETERS

You were introduced to formal parameters earlier. Recall that a formal parameter is a name used to represent an actual value passed to a function. Once again, using the function average as an example:

```
average(amt1, amt2)

     int amt1, amt2;
(
     int answer;
     answer = amt1 + amt2;
     answer = answer/2;
     return(answer);

}
```

amt1 and amt2 are formal parameters.

When you are defining the logic of a function you can think of the formal parameters as local variables. They behave in exactly the same way. For instance, average could be written as:

```
average(amt1,amt2)

    int amt1,amt2;
    {
    amt1 = amt1 + amt2;
    amt1 = amt1/2;
    return(amt1);

}
```

In this version of average the local variable answer was eliminated. Rather, the formal parameter amt1 was used as though it were a local variable.

CALL BY VALUE

— can not change the information

When a function is called, say:

```
n = average(28,42);
```

the actual parameters (28 and 42 in this case) become the values of the formal parameters (amt1 and amt2) in the function definition. Actual parameters are passed to functions using one of two methods: call by value or call by reference. The following analogy seeks to differentiate these two methods.

If you need to know the balance of my bank account, there are two ways I can pass this information to you: I can write the balance on a slip of paper and give you the paper, or I can give you my passbook and let you look up the balance yourself.

In method 1 I'm passing you strictly a value (my balance). It's exactly the information you need. In method 2 I'm passing a reference (my passbook). You can then use the reference to find the value. The first method of passing information illustrates *call by value*. The second method of passing information illustrates *call by reference*.

If I use call by reference, I place my bank balance in some jeopardy—you may use my passbook to make withdrawals! In other words, call by reference affords you the opportunity to change my balance; while call by value affords me protection. By just being told the value of my balance, there is no way you can change it.

When ordinary variables (int, char, float, etc.) are passed to functions, the C compiler arranges for call by value to take place.

Formal Parameters eg. Variable which are used to pass information to a function - "amt1, Can be used as local variables. because they are assigned a value that holds its meaning only within their own function

49

This means that a called function cannot actually change the value of a variable in the calling function. Look at an example:

```
#include <stdio.h>

main()  {

     float bank_bal;   /*local to main*/

     bank_bal = 100.00;
     increase(bank_bal);
     printf("%f", bank_bal);

}

increase(bank_bal)
     float bank_bal;   /*a formal parameter*/
     {
     bank_bal = bank_bal + 500.00;
}
```

NOTE The new value of bank bal can not be returned to main because when increase was called No leading variable "n = increase(bank bal)" was used to allow a value to be returned.

Main's variable bank_bal is local. In increase, bank bal is a formal parameter. Even though the names are the same, they are totally different. If increase was rewritten as:

```
     increase(f) float f; {

          f = f + 500.00;

     }
```

this change would have no affect on the program. Regardless of whether the formal parameter is called "f" or "bank_bal", its use is the same—it is a place holder for the actual argument.

When main calls increase, call by value is used. The C compiler writes "100.00" (the value of bank_bal in main) on a "slip of memory" and passes that slip of memory to increase. Increase changes the slip of memory, but this change has no effect upon main's local variable bank bal. The program prints:

                         100.00

In C, when variables or constants are passed to a function the call by value method is used.

CALL BY REFERENCE

Consider the program that was shown in Exercise 4 of Chapter 1:

```
#include <stdio.h>

main() {

    char line[80];

    printf("Enter a line of text:");
    getline(line, 80);
    printf("%s", line);
}
```

In this program main is calling a function named getline. There are two actual arguments passed: line, and 80.

Because line is an array you know there are really 80 variables named line—line[0], line[1],...,line[79]. How is this information passed to getline?

When an array name is passed to a function, the array name is a reference to the actual array. In other words, arrays are passed using call by reference. Here the call by reference eliminates the task of copying all 80 of the array elements and passing these 80 elements by value. This also means that the called function can actually change the values of the array elements. When the function getline itself is defined, it would begin like this:

```
getline(s,n)
    char s[];     < defines s as a string array variable
    int n;          "   n as an integer
{   /* local variables and logic for getline*/

}
```

The formal parameter:

```
    char s[];
                  is a string array
```

states that s will be a reference to an array of type char. The formal parameter n lets the caller pass an integer to tell getline the size of s.

Call by reference is automatically used by the compiler whenever the name of an array is passed. You will see (Chapter 6) that you can arrange to use call by reference for other data types as well. — using pointers

Let's close this section with an example of call by reference:

```
#include <stdio.h>
main() {
```

```
        char name[4];

        joe(name,4);
        putchar(name[0]);
        putchar(name[1]);
        putchar(name[2]);

}

        joe(s,n)
        char s[];
        int n; {

        s[0] = 'J';
        s[1] = 'o';
        s[2] = 'e';
        s[3] = '\0';   /* end-of-string marker*/

        }
```

[Handwritten annotations: "/* define function called Joe with two arguments */" pointing to joe(name,4); "} print first 3 characters in the array variable called name" bracketing the putchar lines; "end of main →" pointing to the closing brace of main]*

This program prints:

Joe

It illustrates the fact that the function "joe" was actually able to change the value of the local array in main. Whereas variables and constants are passed by value, arrays and strings are always passed by reference.

★STATIC VARIABLES

A few sections back you examined a program to "bump the count." Consider this similar program:

```
#include <stdio.h>

main() {

    int count;

    count = bumpit();
    printf("%d\n", count);

    count = bumpit();
    printf("%d\n", count);

    count = bumpit();
    printf("%d\n", count);

}
bumpit() {
    (auto) int n = 10;
```

[Handwritten annotations: "Define variable 'count' as an integer"; "print value in count"; "— defines n as an integer & sets it to 10. this functions differently than two seperate statements would"; "int n; n = 10;"]

52

```
        n = n + 1;
        return(n);


    }
```

What does this program print? It will print the values that bumpit returns. So let's examine bumpit to see what happens.

In bumpit, n is an automatic variable. The first time bumpit is called, n springs to life, and is initialized to the value 10. Bumpit adds 1 to n and returns the value 11. When bumpit returns to main its automatic variables (n in this case) disappear. So, the first printf call in main prints:

11

On the second call to bumpit the entire cycle repeats. N once again springs to life and is initialized to 10. Again, the value 11 is returned and printed. Therefore, this program prints:

11
11
11

The point to be remembered is that when an atuomatic variable is initialized in a function it is initialized each time the function is called. When the function returns, the automatic variable disappears.

Now consider a slightly different version of the same program:

```
#include <stdio.h>

main() {

    int count;

    count = bumpit();
    printf("%d\n", count);

    count = bumpit();
    printf("%d\n", count);

    count = bumpit();
    printf("%d\n", count);


}

bumpit() {

    static int n = 10;   /* this is different*/
```

If a variable is assigned a value at the same time it is defined and the static storage class is used then the variable will not be reinitalized when the function is called again

53

```
        n = n + 1;

        return(n);

    }
```

The only difference between the two programs is the declaration of the local variable n in bumpit. In this version, the declaration reads:

```
static int n = 10;
```

The C keyword *static* overrides the default *auto*. The variable n is still local to bumpit, but it is no longer automatic; it is static.

Static variables don't appear and disappear like autos, they stick around. So the static int n gets initialized to 10 just once. This happens before bumpit is ever called. On the first call to bumpit 1 is added to n and bumpit returns 11. On the second call n is still holding the value 11. One gets added again and 12 is returned. As a result, this program prints:

$$11$$
$$12$$
$$13$$

You can see now that local variables in functions come in two distinct styles:

1. They can be automatic—they will come and go with calls and returns. If an initializer is present, they are initialized on each call.
2. They can be static—they are initialized once, before the first call. They will retain their value between calls.

*REGISTER VARIABLES

The C keyword *register* is used to enhance a variable's access speed. A declaration of the form:

```
register int i;
```

tells the compiler that "i will be heavily used, store i in a machine register." Ostensibly the program will execute faster if i is in a register rather than memory.

Some C compilers do not implement the keyword register. For those compilers register declarations cannot be made. Further, even when a compiler does implement register, there is no guarantee that a register will be allocated. Because machines have a limited number of registers, only a few registers can be allocated to variables. Use of the register keyword gives guidance to the compiler, not firm direction. Usually the first few register specifications will be honored and the remainder ignored.

Because register refers to actual hardware, not all the data types will fit into a register. Ints and chars will fit. Longs, floats, and doubles won't fit.

★STORAGE CLASSES

When a variable is declared, the full syntax is:

```
storage_class   type   name;
```

as in:

```
register int count;

static char s;

auto int j;
```

The keywords register, static, and auto specify characteristics of the storage that these variables will occupy. In the previous sections we examined what these storage types do. An additional storage type is called extern. Let's take a quick look at *extern*. Consider the following program:

```
#include <stdio.h>
int count;    /* a global variable*/ — initializes count
                                        not initialize count
                     defines count as an
                          integer variable
main() {

    count = setcount();  ← calls function setcount()
    printf("%d\n", count);

}

int init_count = 1;   /* another global variable*/
                     defines variable as an integer and
setcount() {               sets it to 1

    return(init_count);  returns the value of init_count
                          as the result of running setcount

}
```

In this program both count and init_count are global variables. However, main cannot access init_count because init_count is defined further down in the program. The scope of a global variable is from the point in the source file where it is defined to the end of the source file.

Total program simply prints the number 1

If main needed access to init_count the function main could begin like this:

```
main(){

    extern init_count;

        .
        .
        .

}
```

The declaration:

extern init_count;

says that init_count is a global variable defined later on. It could be defined later in the same source file, or it might be defined in another file altogether. We'll return to this issue in Chapter 9.

Another way to provide main access to init count is to move its declaration near the top of the file. For instance, the program could start:

```
#include <stdio.h>

int count;

int init_count;

main() {

        .
        .
        .

}
```

Now all the functions in this file have access to the global variables count and init_count.

TYPICAL ORGANIZATION OF A C PROGRAM

With the preceding background on variables and functions, consider Fig. 3-3, which illustrates the organization of a typical C program. This organization is typical when the entire program is in one source file; programs that span several source files are discussed in Chapter 9.

At the beginning of the program, preprocessor statements are used. For example, a #include statement is used to include

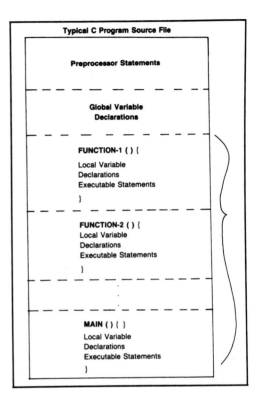

Fig. 3-3. A Typical
C Program File.

the I/O header file, and #define statements can be used to define symbolic constants.

Also near the beginning of the program are global variable declarations. By placing these declarations near the beginning of the program all functions within the file can access them without making further declarations.

Next are function definitions with each function declaring its own formal parameters and local variables. In each C program there is exactly one function named main. Figure 3-4 shows a small program that adheres to this organization.

In Fig. 3-4 the function main is shown last. This need not be the case; the functions can be defined in any order, but function order can cause additional declarations to be required. When a function calls another function the compiler needs to know the type of value the called function will return. If the function has yet to be defined the compiler assumes it will return an int. If the called function does not return int, a declaration must be made stating the type of value the function returns. The following short program illustrates this:

```
main() {

    double y;
```

```
        double square();   /* must declare square */

        y = square(2.0);
        printf("%f",y);

}

double square(x)
        double x;

{

        return(x * x);

}
```

In this program main calls the function *square*. Since the call is made before the function square is defined, you must declare that square returns a double. If the order of the functions is reversed the declaration is no longer required. This is illustrated by the following program:

```
#include <stdio.h>

average( amt1, amt2 )
        int amt1, amt2;
{
        int answer;

        answer = amt1 + amt2;
        answer = answer / 2;
        return(answer);
}

main()
{
        int n = 10;
        int m = 78;
        int ave;

        ave = average(n, m);
        printf("The average of %d and %d is %d \n", n, m, ave);
}
```

Fig. 3-4. Sample organization of a typical C Program.

```
                                    Tells the type of variable to be returned
                                      when the function is called
double square(x)
     double x;   Defines the variable x as a
                    double prescision
(                      floating point number

     return (x * x);  < multiply x times x

}

main() {
     double y;
     y = square(2.0);
     printf("%f",y);

}
```

With this function order the compiler knows the function square returns a double prior to the call made by main. With this order you need not declare the function square.

Figure 3-3 gave you an idea of how a C program will look. Significant variation from this organization will occur, but the figure provides a starting point. The examples in Chapter 5 use and build upon this program organization.

EXERCISES

1. Define a null function named "example" that
   a. Has three arguments, a char, an int, and an int; and returns an int.

   b. Has one argument—a double—and returns a double.

   c. Has two arguments, both ints, and returns no values.

2. Enter the program in Fig. 3-2 into your system, compile it, link it, and run it.
   a. What does it print? Is it correct?

   b. Using your text editor, edit the first line of main to read:
   ```
   int n= 113;
   ```

   Recompile and relink. Run the new program. What does it print? Is it correct? What can you conclude about division of integers?

3. Write a clear_screen function that will work for your terminal. Write a function called "home" that will clear the screen and move the cursor to the top row, first column. Identify other terminal functions you can write for your terminal and write them.

4. Using the following main function:

```
#define NAMESIZE 20
main() {

        int j = 0;
        int m;
        char s = 'a';
        char t;
        char name[NAMESIZE];
m = funca(j);   /* CALL 1*/
t = funcb(s);   /* CALL 2*/
m = funcc(name);   /* CALL 3*/
m = funcd(name[0]);   /* CALL 4*/

}
```

a. Classify each of the four function calls as "call by value" or "call by reference."

b. Write null functions that specify the return type and formal parameters for funca, funcb, funcc, and funcd.

5. In the following C program, identify the
   a. local variables
   b. global variables, and
   c. formal parameters:

```
int value = 15;
int tolerance = 1;
main() {

      int answer;

      answer = calculate(value,tolerance);
      printf("%d", answer);

}

calculate(v,t)
      int v,t;

{

      int j;
      j = v+t;
      return(j);

}
```

See p. 73 for summary
p. 83

Chapter 4

Assignment, Arithmetic and Relational Operators

You've examined an overview of C. You've examined the environment. You can declare variables and define functions. In this chapter you'll see how to combine and transform the values contained in the variables. *Operators* are the language elements that perform these transformations.

OPERATORS, EXPRESSIONS, AND STATEMENTS

Operators perform actions. The objects that operators act upon are called *operands*. For example, the well known addition operator (+) acts upon two operands. This is exemplified by notation such as: 3 + 5, which means "perform the addition operation on the operands 3 and 5." The result of this operation produces the value 8.

Operators can be categorized by the number of operands they require. A *unary* operator acts upon one operand, a *binary* operator acts upon two operands, and a *ternary* operator acts upon three operands. For instance, in the above example 3 + 5 indicates that + is a binary operator.

As we discuss operators we'll use the terms *expression* and *statement*. Simply defined, an expression is a sequence of operands and operators. For example:

```
5
10 + 20
rate * time
c = getchar()
```

are all expressions. The first two are constant expressions—
their values never change. The last three expressions contain
operators (+,*, and =) in addition to operands (10,20,rate,
time,c, and getchar()). Here, you see that constants, variables,
and function calls can all serve as operands in expressions.

In C, all expressions share a common property; every
expression has a value. In the expressions:

```
5
10 + 20
c = getchar()
```
✗

the first expression has the value "5," the second "30," the third
has whatever value is returned by getchar(), and the fourth has
the value currently stored in variable x.

There is another property of expressions that is not
universally shared. Some expressions name memory locations,
while others do not. For instance, if z and s are declared as:

```
int z;       define variable z as an 'integer
int s[10];        s as    "    "    array size of 10
```

then the expressions:

```
z
s[3]
```

both name memory locations. On the other hand, the expressions:

```
z + 1
s[4] + 2
```

do not name memory locations. In C, expressions that name
memory locations are called *lvalues*. Some operators require
that their operands be lvalue expressions. We'll discuss this
further as the need arises.

A *statement* is an expression terminated by a semicolon.
For example:

```
c = getchar()
```

l value = Location Value

is an expression, whereas:

```
c = getchar();
```

is a statement. The semicolon is the C *statement terminator*.

With this background information and these working definitions, let's look at the assignment, arithmetic and relational operators.

THE SIMPLE ASSIGNMENT OPERATOR

The equal sign is the

The simple assignment operator is used to move the value of an expression into a memory location. The operator is denoted by an equals sign (=). For instance, in the statement:

```
x = 5;
```

the value five is placed into the variable x. As you know, x names a memory location. In:

```
rate = 0.175;
time = now;
```

the first statement assigns rate the value 0.175, and the second assigns time the current value of the variable now. We've called this *simple* assignment to distinguish it from *operational* assignment, a concept we'll discuss later in this chapter.

Multiple assignments can occur in one statement, as in:

```
x=y=z=0;
```

The assignments are performed from right to left, so z is assigned zero, y is assigned the value of z (which is now zero), etc. The result is that x,y, and z are all assigned the value zero.

In a more formal (and a bit more abstract) sense the assignment operator is a binary operator. It uses two operands and is denoted as:

```
left_expression = right_expression
```

Right expression can be any expression. For instance:

```
x = y * 3.0 + z[15];
```

will cause the expression on the right of the assignment operator to be evaluated, and the resulting value will be stored at the memory location named x. Left expression is more re-

63

stricted. It must be an expression that names a memory location (an lvalue). At this point you've seen only two ways to name memory locations—variable names and array elements. Hence, the left expression in:

```
z = y + 2;
```

and:

```
count[7] = curcount + 1;
```

both name memory locations and are valid operands for the assignment operator.

We've injected this extra formalism into the discussion for two reasons: In subsequent chapters you will see other ways to name memory locations. With this additional information left expressions will become much more complex than just a variable name or array element. Also, understanding this formalism may help you understand some of the error messages your C compiler provides. Many C compilers will issue compilation error messages of the form:

name is not an lvalue

This error will occur if you use an expression on the left side of an assignment operation which does not name a memory location.

As one last bit of formalism, notice that an expression such as:

```
x = y
```

actually implies three values—the value of y, the value of x, and the value of the expression x = y. In the case of assignment, the value of y is assigned to x and that value becomes the value of the expression. We'll return to this distinction when we discuss relational operators.

ARITHMETIC OPERATORS

To perform arithmetic, C provides the binary operators + (addition), - (subtraction), * (multiplication), / (division), and % (the modulus operator). These operators are used in expressions like:

```
x + y    /*add value of x to value of y */

rate * time   /*multiply value of rate times
                  value of time*/
```

64

```
miles/gallon /*divide value of miles
                 by the value of gallons*/
etc.
```

When the division operator is used with integer operands, an integer result is provided. Any fractional portion of the result is discarded. For example, Listing 4-1 prints:

```
the result of 7/2 is 3
```

because the fractional portion is discarded for integer division.

The modulus operator (%) is used with integer operands (int, short, long, unsigned). It cannot be used with float or double operands. The modulus operator is used to find the remainder that would be obtained when its left operand is divided by its right operand. For instance, in the statement:

```
y = 7 % 2;
```

y is assigned the value one, because one is the remainder obtained from the integer division of 7 by 2. In:

```
z = 100 % 10;
```

z is assigned the value zero because the remainder of dividing 100 by 10 is zero. In general, if x and y are integers and x divides y evenly, then:

```
y % x
```

has the value zero.

Program Listing 4-2 illustrates the use of some of the arithmetic and assignment operators. It converts a large number

Listing 4-1. Example of division operator used with integer operands.

```
#include <stdio.h>

main() {

        int quot, div, result;

        quot = 7;
        div = 2;
        result = quot/div;
        printf("The result of %d / %d is ", quot, div );
        printf("%d",result);

}
```

alue of the entire expression

Listing 4-2. Example of arithmetic and assignment operators.

```
#define INCHES_PER_MILE 63360L
#define INCHES_PER_YARD 36
#define INCHES_PER_FOOT 12

#include <stdio.h>

main() {

        long inches, miles, yards, feet;

        /*start with a bunch of inches */
        inches = 3281931L;
        printf(" %ld inches is:\n", inches);

        /* determine the number of miles */
        miles = inches / INCHES_PER_MILE;
        inches = inches % INCHES_PER_MILE;

        /* determine the number of yards */
        yards = inches / INCHES_PER_YARD;
        inches = inches % INCHES_PER_YARD;

        /* determine the number of feet */
        feet = inches / INCHES_PER_FOOT;
        inches = inches % INCHES_PER_FOOT;

        /* the remainder from the last modulus operation is the
           correct number of inches   */

        printf("\t %ld miles, %ld yards, ", miles, yards);
        printf(" %ld feet, %ld inches\n", feet, inches);

    }
```

of inches into miles, yards, feet, and inches. For instance, starting out with 1768 inches, it would print:

```
1768 inches is:
0 miles, 49 yards, 4 inches.
```

In order to hold a large number of inches, we used the long integer data type.

A couple of points can be made about this program. First, the #define statements are used to give descriptive names to numeric constants used in the program. Secondly, when determining how many miles are expressed, we used the statement:

miles = inches/INCHES_PER_MILE;

As you know, the token INCHES_PER_MILE is replaced with the long constant 63360L by the preprocessor. Since the statement represents integer division, any fractional portion of the division is thrown away. Hence we have the number of whole miles contained in the value of the variable *inches.*

Now the statement:

```
inches = inches%INCHES_PER_MILE;
```

says "take the remainder left over when inches is divided by INCHES_PER_MILE and assign the remainder's value back into inches." This value represents the fractional miles. Using the same approach the conversion is made into yards then to feet. This program prints:

```
3281931 inches is:  51 miles, 1404 yards, 2 feet, 3 inches
```

UNARY MINUS, INCREMENT, AND DECREMENT OPERATORS

Unary operators are those operators which use only one operand. C provides a unary minus operator (-), an *increment operator* (++), and a *decrement operator* (--). The unary minus changes the sign of its operand. For instance, -x will have the value -2 if x has value two, and two if x has value -2. C does not have a unary plus operator.

The increment operator (++) adds one to its operand. The decrement operator subtracts one from its operand. For example:

```
count++;
```

is equivalent to writing:

```
count = count+1;
```

Similarly:

```
size--;
```

is equivalent to:

```
size = size-1;
```

Analogous to the discussion of left expressions and assignment, the increment and decrement operators can only be applied to variable names, array elements, and other expressions that actually name memory locations. For instance:

```
x++;
count++;
rate[3]++;
```

are all valid statements. The statements:

```
(rate * time)++;   /* WRONG */
(x/y)++;   /* WRONG */
```

are illegal because the parenthesized expressions do not refer to memory locations.

The ++ and -- operators can be written either before the variable as in:

```
++x
```

or after the variable, as in:

```
x++
```

The first example is called *prefix notation,* the second is called *postfix notation.* There is a difference between the two forms.

In prefix notation the variable is incremented (or decremented) before its value is taken. In postfix notation, the variable is incremented (or decremented) after its value is taken. For example, in:

```
x = 7;
printf("%d",x++);
y = x;
```

seven is the value printed, then x is incremented and the value eight is assigned to y. In:

```
x = 7;
printf("%d",++x);
y = x;
```

x is incremented before its value is taken, hence eight is printed and the value eight is assigned to y. In a statement like:

```
i++;
```

where the only purpose of the increment operator is to increment a variable, either prefix or postfix notation can be used. The choice is a matter of personal style. However, in statements like:

```
j = ++i;   /* Prefix notation */
```

or

```
j = i++;   /* Postfix notation */
```

the two forms produce a different result. If i has the value of five, the prefix example above will assign five to j then increment i to the value six. The postfix example will increment i to six and assign six to j.

Similarly, if i's value is five, the statement:

```
y = x[i++];
```

assigns the value of x[5] to y and increments i to six. The statement:

```
y = x[++i];
```

increments i to six and assigns the value of x[6] to y.

OPERATIONAL ASSIGNMENT OPERATORS

Operational assignment describes a group of C operators that perform both an operation and an assignment. These operators have the form "op=", where *op* can be any of the C binary operators. For instance, +=, *=, /=, and %= are all operational assignment operators.

The statement:

```
x += 5;
```

means "add five to x and assign the result to x." This statement is equivalent to:

```
x = x + 5;
```

The following three statements are all equivalent:

```
x += 1;
x++;
x = x + 1;
```

The statement:

```
rate *= 100.0;
```

is equivalent to the statement:

```
rate = rate * 100.0;
```

Though the term "operational assignment" is descriptive of what these operators do, they are generally just called *assign-*

ment operators. These operators can save considerable typing. For instance, typing:

```
counter[curval] += 5;
```

is considerably faster than typing:

```
counter[curval] = counter[curval] + 5;
```

Also, if the expression to be operated upon is complex, the operational assignment operators can help to eliminate hard-to-find errors. For example, in the following statement an array element is indexed by a fairly complex expression. The intent is to add the value of a variable "curcount" to that array element:

```
counter[offset + position[i*j] * factor] =
        counter[offset + position[1*j] * factor] + curcount;
```

We have made an error in indexing the position array in the second part of the statement (1*j rather than i*j). The chance of making such an error is eliminated by the operational assignment form:

```
counter[offset + position[i*j] * factor] += curcount;
```

In the formal sense, the expression:

```
left_expr op= expression
```

is equivalent to:

```
left_expr = (left_expr) op (expression)
```

The parentheses can make a difference. For instance:

```
r *= s + t;
```

means:

```
r = (r) *(s + t);
```

This last statement is different from:

```
r = r * s + t;
```

because multiplication is performed before addition. We'll discuss the order of evaluation in the next section.

70

In addition to the binary operators you have already examined $(+,-,*,/,\%)$, the operational assignment form can be used with the bitwise operators that we will discuss in Chapter 9.

As an example of the operational assignment operators, compare Listing 4-3 to convert inches with the version written previously.

OPERATOR PRECEDENCE

Expressions like $2+3*6$ can be ambiguous. If performed left to right the result is 30 $(2+3=5,\ 5*6=30)$, while if performed right to left the result is 20. To make such expressions unambiguous rules are added to the language defining the order in which operations will be performed. These rules are formed by giving each operator a precedence. An operator having a higher precedence is performed before one having a lower precedence. When arithmetic operators have equal precedence, they are generally performed from left to right.

Listing 4-3. Example of operational assignment operators.

```
        #define INCHES_PER_MILE 63360L
        #define INCHES_PER_YARD 36
        #define INCHES_PER_FOOT 12

        #include <stdio.h>

        main() {

                long inches, miles, yards, feet;

                /*start with a bunch of inches */
                inches = 3281931L;
                printf(" %ld inches is:\n", inches);

                /* determine the number of miles */
                miles = inches / INCHES_PER_MILE;
                inches %= INCHES_PER_MILE;

                /* determine the number of yards */
                yards = inches / INCHES_PER_YARD;
                inches %= INCHES_PER_YARD;

                /* determine the number of feet */
                feet = inches / INCHES_PER_FOOT;
                inches %= INCHES_PER_FOOT;

                /* the remainder from the last modulus operation is the
                   correct number of inches  */

                printf("\t %ld miles, %ld yards, ", miles, yards);
                printf(" %ld feet, %ld inches\n", feet, inches);

        }
```

Of the operators you have seen so far, the unary operators (-, ++, --) have the highest precedence. Next in precedence are the multiplication, division, and modulus operators (*, /, %). These are followed by the addition and subtraction operators (+, -). Finally, the assignment operators (=, +=, *=, etc.) have the lowest precedence. These rules imply that the expression:

```
a + b * c
```

means:

```
a + (b * c)
```

where the parentheses show that the multiplication is performed before the addition. Multiplication is performed first because its precedence is higher than that of addition. Similarity, the expression:

```
x + --y * z
```

means:

```
x + ((--y) * z )
```

When parentheses are nested, as they are in this case, the order of evaluation is determined by working from the innermost set of parentheses out. In the last expression the decrement operator has the highest precedence so it is performed first. It is shown enclosed in the innermost parentheses. Next the multiplication is performed, and lastly the addition.

The order of evaluation determined by the precedence of the operators can be overridden. To do this you must use parentheses in the expression to explicitly force a particular order. For instance:

```
y = (a + b) * c;
```

forces addition to occur before multiplication even though the precedence of multiplication is higher than the precedence of addition.

There is still the question of what happens when all the operators in an expression have the same precedence. For instance, how is the expression:

```
10 - 6 - 2
```

evaluated? This question is answered by considering the way in

72

which operators associate with their operands.

By *associate* we mean "how will the compiler group operands about the operators in the absence of explicit parentheses?" In C, most of the binary operators will associate left to right. With left-to-right associativity, the above expression means:

```
(10 - 6) - 2
```

Here we started on the left, grouping operands about the operators while moving to the right. This expression has the value two.

Just like precedence, operator associativity can be overridden by using parentheses to force the association you want. For example, in the expression:

```
10 - (6 - 2)
```

the parentheses force a different association than the one above. This expression has the value six.

Table 4-1 summarizes the precedence and associativity of the operators we have discussed so far. In the table the operators are grouped according to their precedence. Operators having the highest precedence are at the top of the table. Operators between the horizontal lines have the same precedence and associativity. The last column of the table shows how operands are associated with the operators when parentheses are not used.

Notice that function calls and array references are evaluated before arithmetic operations are performed. This means that in an expression like:

```
square(y) + square(x)
```

the function calls are made before the addition is performed.

Table 4-1 Precedence of the Arithmetic Operators.

Operator Use	Operator Symbol	Associativity
function calls array references	() []	Left To Right
urinary minus increment, decrement	— →mean change sign ++ −−	Right To Left
multiply, divide modulus	* / %	Left To Right
add, subtract	+ −	Left To Right
assignment	= += *= /= −= %=	Right To Left

Similarly, in:

```
value[i] * value[i+1]
```

the array references are resolved before multiplication is performed. Notice in Table 4-1 that the assignment operators are at the bottom of the precedence totem pole. This guarantees that in expressions like:

```
x = y * r % t - d
```

assignment is the very last thing to occur. Thus, all the calculations implied by the operators on the right side of the assignment operator are performed before the assignment takes place.

★CAVEATS ON ORDER OF EVALUATION

Operators like ★ and + satisfy mathematical properties called *associativity* and *commutativity*. As before, the term associativity relates to how operands are grouped. In this context associativity means that the result of a series of operations does not depend on the way in which operands are grouped. For instance, 3★2★4 equals 24 regardless of whether it is evaluated as (3★2)★4 or 3★(2★4). This is because ★ is an associative operator. Note that (16/4)/2 does not equal 16/(4/2), since division is not an associative operator.

Commutativity means the order of the operands does not affect the result of the operation. For instance, 4+2 equals 2+4 since addition is a commutative operation. However, 4 - 2 does not equal 2 -4 since subtraction is not commutative.

When an operator is both commutative and associative, C does not guarantee the order of evaluation. Thus, an expression written as p★r★t may be evaluated as (p★r)★t, or it may be evaluated as p★(r★t). This is true even when parentheses are used. For instance, if you write:

```
result = (p*r)*t;
```

it might actually be evaluated as:

```
result = p*(r*t);
```

This rarely matters, but if for some reason the first order of evaluation must be maintained, the statement should be broken into two parts, as in:

```
temp = p*r;
result=temp*t;
```

One last caveat about the order of evaluation within expressions: when functions are called, the order in which the function arguments are evaluated is not guaranteed. For example, consider:

```
n = 0;
printf("%d %d", ++n, ++n,);
```

This call to the function printf is not guaranteed to print "1 2" as you might think it would. "1 2" will be printed if the arguments to printf are evaluated in the order they are listed. C does not guarantee that this will happen. Consequently, you should be careful when you pass to function arguments which require evaluations. Make sure that the order in which the arguments are evaluated does not matter. When in doubt, perform the evaluation outside the function call. For instance, for the above example, the program fragment:

```
n = 0;
m = n++; p = n++;
printf("%d %d", m,p);
```

will print: "1 2".

ARITHMETIC WITH CHAR DATA TYPE

As you would expect, the arithmetic operators can be used on the numeric data types (int, long, short, float, etc.) but they can be used on other types as well. For instance, it is permissable to use the arithmetic operators on character data. For example, consider the function upper which converts a lowercase ASCII letter to its corresponding uppercase letter (Listing 4–4). This function works because in the ASCII character set values of lowercase and uppercase letters are separated by a constant amount of 32 (see Table 2–2). For instance, the character a is represented in ASCII by the decimal value 97, while the character A is represented by the value 65. You can easily transform lowercase ASCII characters to uppercase by using the subtraction operator.

As another example of the usefulness of arithmetic on characters, consider the expression:

```
s - '0'
```

where s is a char variable and '0' is the character constant zero. If

Listing 4-4. Converting lowercase ASCII to uppercase.

```
upper(letter) char letter; {

        /* convert lower case ASCII to upper case */

    char u;
    u = letter - 32;
    return (u);

}
```

you refer to Table 2-2 you see that the decimal value of '0' is 48. The Table 4-2 illustrates the value of s - '0' when various ASCII characters are stored in s. As you can see, the expression

$$s - \,'0'$$ *numerical digit*

has the effect of converting an ASCII digit to its corresponding numeric value.

ARITHMETIC WITH UNSIGNED DATA TYPES

When arithmetic operations are used on the unsigned types, these operations obey the rules of "arithmetic modulo n."

In normal, everyday arithmetic, when two positive operands are added the result is larger than either operand. Because in theory there is no such thing as the "largest possible integer," no problems result.

Within a computer there is a largest possible integer. For instance, if 16 bits of storage are used to store unsigned values, then 2^{16} or (65536) different values can be stored. Hence, only the unsigned integers 0,1,2,...,65535 can be represented in storage.

If the sum (or product) of two unsigned integers exceeds the largest possible unsigned value, the result is determined according to the rules of *arithmetic modulo n*. Arithmetic modulo n is like arithmetic on a circle. Consider Fig. 4-1, where

Table 4-2. Values of ASCII Characters Stored in S.

ASCII Character Stored in s	Decimal Value of s	Decimal Value of '0'	Decimal Value of s — '0'
'0'	48	48	0
'1'	49	48	1
'2'	50	48	2
'3'	51	48	3
'4'	52	48	4
'5'	53	48	5

76

seven distinct integers (0,1,2,3,4,5,and 6) are drawn in a circle. We'll use the figure to illustrate arithmetic modulo 7. The addition of 3 + 4 (modulo 7) can be carried out on the circle at the top of the figure by positioning your finger on 3, then moving four points clockwise. So, 3 + 4 equals zero in modulo 7 arithmetic. Similarly, 5 + 6 equals four (modulo 7).

Subtraction is performed on the circle at the bottom of the figure by moving counter-clockwise. For example, 4 - 6 equals five (modulo 7). In this particular arithmetic, seven is called the modulus. These answers may seem counter-intuitive, but notice that such counter-intuitive answers only occur when the result exceeds the modulus or would be negative. For instance:

```
1 + 3 = 4 (modulo 7)

6 - 5 = 1 (modulo 7)
```

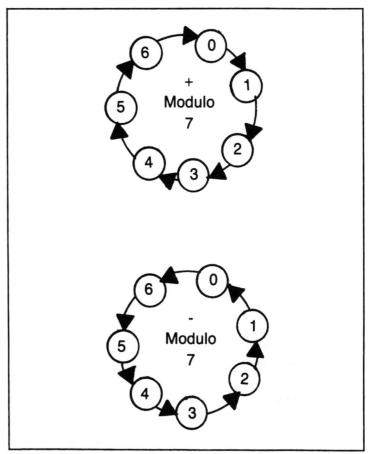

Fig. 4-1. Arithmetic Modulo 7.

The important thing to note is that an arithmetic operation modulo 7 always produces a nonnegative result in the range of 0-6.

In C, unsigned arithmetic is performed modulo N, where N is the maximum number of distinct unsigned values (such as 2^{16}). Thus, any arithmetic operation on unsigned variables will produce an unsigned result in the proper range.

★TYPE CONVERSIONS

It is permissible to mix types in arithmetic expressions. For instance, if count is of type int, and number is of type float, an expression like:

```
number * count
```

is allowed. There is some question as to the value and type of the result in this case.

When an operator acts upon operands of different types, how is the result produced? Zahn's notion of the "widening hierarchy" [ZAHN 79] is useful here. The C data types can be ordered into a widening hierarchy from char to double. This is shown in Fig. 4-2. The figure indicates that double is the widest data type, char is the narrowest, float is wider than int, and so on. To say that long is wider than char implies that a long value occupies more storage than a char value.

When two operands have different types, a type conversion takes place. The value of the narrower operand is converted to a wider type. For instance, if c is a char and i is an int, then in:

```
c + i
```

c is converted to int before the addition operation takes place. Since int is the wider of the two types, no information is lost in the calculation.

It is not uncommon for C compilers to perform conversions to types wider than required. In fact the UNIX C compilers always convert char to int and float to double before these types are operated upon.

In general, when data types are mixed in expressions, sensible conversions are made. Precision is lost only if a wide data type is assigned to a narrower one. For instance, assigning a float to an int will cause the loss of the fractional information.

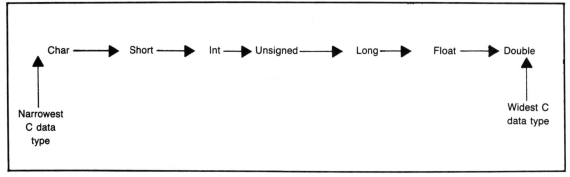

Fig. 4-2. The Widening Hierarchy of C Data Types.

CAST AND SIZEOF OPERATORS

Type conversions can be explicitly requested in C by using a construct called the *type cast* (or *cast*) operator. The cast operator is written by enclosing the name of a C data type in parentheses. For instance, the expression:

```
(float)(i * k)
```

explicitly requests that the value of i * k be converted to type float. In the literature surrounding UNIX and C this is called type coercion. It is said that the value of i * k is *coerced* to the type float.

The cast operator is useful in passing information to functions. For instance, consider a function named exp which has been defined as:

```
double exp(z) double z; {

        /* logic of exp*/

    }
```

You can see that exp is expecting a double as an argument. Using the cast operator, you can call exp with an integer variable n as follows: exp ((double)n); The cast operator causes n to be converted to a double, and the double value is passed to the function exp.

We have mentioned that the size of objects (chars, ints, floats, etc.) will vary from machine to machine. In C an operator called *sizeof* is available so that programs can determine the size of things. For instance, the statement:

```
n = sizeof(double);
```

79

will assign to the variable n the size of the type double. The size is returned in bytes.

In general, the expression:

```
sizeof(type)
```

will return the number of bytes of storage used by the specified type. Type can be any of the data types you've seen so far (int, char, long, etc.). It can also be used to find the size of arrays, structures (Chapter 7), and unions (Chapter 9). We'll discuss this further in later chapters.

RELATIONAL OPERATORS

When writing programs you will want to compare various data within the program. For instance, a game program may wish to compare a variable called score to one called max_score to determine if the current player has set a new scoring record. To do this you must test whether the relationship "score is greater than max score" is true.

Relationships can be expressed in C by using the relational operators. These operators are $>$ (greater than), $>=$ (greater than or equal to), $<$ (less than), $<=$ (less than or equal to), $==$ (equal to), and $!=$ (not equal to). They are summarized in Table 4-3. Notice that some of the relational operators are written using two characters; for example, the not equal operator is an exclamation point followed by an equal sign. Spaces are not allowed between these two characters. Also note that the operator which tests for equality is written as two equal signs. This distinguishes it from the assignment operator.

Relations imply a logical assertion. If you write:

```
x >= y
```

you make an assertion that "x is greater than or equal to y." This assertion may be true or it may be false. Its truth value depends

Table 4-3. C Relational Operators.

Operator Symbol	Operator Use	Example
==	Test for equality	x == y
!=	Test for inequality	x != y
>	Test for greater than	x > y
>=	Test for greater than or equal to	x >= y
<	Test for less than	x < y
<=	Test for less than or equal to	x <= y

on the values of x and y at the time the expression x>=y is evaluated. Expressions that use relational operators have a value of one if the relation is true, or zero if the relation is false. For instance, if i has the value 10, and j has the value 8, then the expressions.

```
i >= j
i > j
```

are both true, so their value is one. The expressions:

```
i == j
i < j
```

are both false, so their value is zero.

If s is a character array holding the string "the," and t is a character array holding the string "thy," then:

```
s[0] == t[0] is true (value 1)
s[1] == t[1] is true (value 1)
s[2] == t[2] is false (value 0)    /*s[2]=='e' but
                                      t[2] =='y' */
s[3] == t[3] is true (value 1)
```

Recall that strings are terminated by the null character ('\0'), so s[3] and t[3] are in fact equal.

When you test to see if a character array element contains the end-of-string marker there are several ways the relational expression can be phrased. For instance, any of the following expressions is correct:

```
s[j] == NULL          /* assuming: #define NULL 0 */
s[j] == 0
s[j] == '\0'
```

The last form is most often used. Since '\0' is a character constant whose value is zero, this form emphasizes that you are dealing with characters.

Since a relational expression has a value you can combine it with an assignment operator as follows:

```
z = (i >= j)
```

In this expression z is assigned the value one if i >= j is true.

It is assigned the value (0 if i >= j is false.

The operands of a relational operator can, of course, be expressions. For instance, you can assert:

```
(x + 15) > 20
```

in which case the expression on the left (x + 15) will be evaluated and compared to 20. If the value of x + 15 is greater than 20 the relational expression is true and its value is one.

When we introduced the assignment operator, we made a point to inject the fact that an assignment expression has a value. This fact is frequently used in combination with relational operators. For instance:

```
(s[i] = t[i]) != '\0'
```

is a common C idiom. The expression on the left (s[i] = t[i]) is *evaluated*. Because the assignment operator is used, evaluation just means "assign the value of t[i] to s[i]." Now this value (the value of the assignment expression) is compared to '\0'. If it is not '\0', the relational expression is true (value one); otherwise, it is false (value zero). If s and t are strings, the net effect of this expression is to copy the character stored in t[i] into s[i], then check to see if the end-of-string marker was copied. You will see such constructions frequently in the next chapter.

It is also very common in C for one of the operands of a relational expression to be a function call rather than a variable. For instance, consider:

```
getchar()!=EOF
```

In this expression getchar is called to fetch an input character. The character so fetched is then compared to EOF (the symbolic constant for end-of-file). If the value returned by getchar is different from EOF, this expression is true and the value of the expression is one. If EOF is returned by getchar, this expression is false and its value is zero. Again, the relational expression has a value of one or zero, meaning true or false respectively. Because relational expressions that perform character processing are so common in C, let's examine another example.

In the expression:

```
( c = getchar() ) != EOF
```

evaluation proceeds from inside the parentheses. Getchar is called and its returned value is assigned to the variable c. That value is then compared to EOF. If c does not equal EOF, this expression is true. If c does equal EOF, the expression is false. In either event the character that getchar fetched was saved in c.

Notice the difference between:

[handwritten margin notes:] equal sign is the assignment expression see p.63 and that value is equal to the value of the right side of the = sign, after it has been evaluated.

[handwritten notes:] this does ← statement. Two things at once in: 1. sets c equal to input from keyboard 2. Check to see if the key pressed was the null character & 3. set the value of the expression to 1 or zero depending on the result

```
            c = getchar() != EOF              example _
```

and

```
            (c = getchar() ) != EOF           example 2
```

Because relational operators have a higher precedence than assignment operators the expression in example 1 is evaluated as:

```
            c = (getchar() != EOF)
```

This order of evaluation causes getchar to fetch a character, compare the character to EOF, then assign c the value one if EOF was not read, or zero if EOF was read. The character fetched by getchar is not assigned to a variable. If you wish to force an assignment operator to take precedence over a relational operator (as in example 2 above), parentheses must be used. The construction in example 2 should be memorized as it is a very common and useful expression.

Table 4-4 updates Table 4-1 to show where the relational operators fit into the precedence hierarchy. Also shown in Table

Table 4-4 Precedence of the Arithmetic And Relational Operators.

Operator Use	Operator Symbol	Associativity
function calls array references	() []	Left To Right
unary minus increment, decrement cast, sizeof negation	– ++ –– (type) sizeof !	Right To Left
multiply, divide modulus	* / %	Left To Right
add, subtract	+ –	Left To Right
relational	< <= > >=	Left To Right
equality, inequality	== !=	Left To Right
logical connective and	&&	Left To Right
logical connective or	||	Left To Right
conditional	?:	Right To Left
assignment	= += –= *= /= %=	Right To Left

Note: Operators between horizontal bars have same precedence and associativity. Top of table is the highest precedence operators.

83

[handwritten annotations: * order of exicution, 1 2 3 4 5 6 7 8 9 10, ..for file, – means change sign, ! means change truth value, Compare, AND, OR, If then Else, Let or set, of the comparason. * If two or more operators of same level are used you must use parentises to force c to perform them in the order you wish! see p.75]

4-4 is the precedence of the logical connectives, the negation operator, and the :? conditional operator. We'll discuss the latter operators shortly.

LOGICAL CONNECTIVES

Various relations can be combined by the logical connectives && (the logical AND operator) and || (the logical OR operator). The assertion:

```
expression-1 && expression-2
```

is true when both expression-1 and expression-2 are non-zero. Note that any non-zero value is considered true. As you have seen, when the compiler must supply a value for true it uses the value one, which is certainly nonzero.

The assertion:

```
expression-1 || expression-2
```

is true when either expression-1 or expression-2 (or both) is nonzero. The character used to represent the logical OR operator appears on the keyboard as a vertical bar. On some terminal keyboards the vertical bar is solid while on others it has a break in the middle. The character is typed twice to represent the logical or operator.

A common use of logical connectives in C is the test for white space. *White space* is the name given to those characters (spaces, tabs, and newlines) that produce blank space on a printed page. The test looks like this:

```
c == '\t' || c == ' ' || c == '\n'
```

== means to evaluate is leftside = to right side & return value 1 = yes, 0 = No

This expression is true when the value of c is either the tab, space, or new line character. Using logical connectives, you can test to see if a variable c holds a lowercase ASCII alphabetic character by the expression:

```
'a' <= c && c <= 'z'
```

p. 44

Since the precedence of the logical connectives is lower than the precedence of the relational operator (refer to Table 4-4), the expression can be written without parentheses. To find out if an integer variable j is between 1 and 100, you can write:

because the size comparisons will be made before the two sides are anded together.

```
1 < j && j < 100
```

Note that the logical connectives are required to perform these types of tests. For instance, the expression:

```
1 < j < 100      /* WRONG */
```

will not correctly test that j is between 1 and 100. Suppose j equals 500; in this case the last expression would be evaluated left to right as:

```
(1 < 500) < 100
      1 < 100
      TRUE
```

Since $1 < 500$ is true, the value of the expression $(1 < 500)$ is 1. And certainly $1 < 100$ is true, so the expression $1 < j < 100$ is true even when j equals 500.

As further examples of using logical connectives, consider:

```
x < xlimit && y < ylimit
```

which is true only when both $x < xlimit$ and $y < ylimit$ are true. The expression:

```
found && morespace
```

uses two variables to form a logical expression. The expression is true if both found and morespace have non-zero values. The expression:

```
x == 0 || y == 0
```

is true if either x or y is equal to zero.

When an expression using the connective && or || is evaluated, it is evaluated from left to right. The evaluation stops as soon as the truth or falsehood of the entire expression is known. If x is equal to zero, then the truth of the expression:

```
x==0 || y==0
```

is determined when the $x == 0$ test is made. Hence, y is not tested for equality to zero. This fact can be extremely important when writing relational expressions that produce "side effects." For instance, consider:

```
x==y || --x==0
```

When this expression is evaluated from left to right, if x equals y the truth of the entire expression is known. Hence the condition --x equal to zero is not tested. The side effect of decrementing x only occurs when x does not equal y.

As another example, consider:

[handwritten margin note: read is x equal zero or y equal zero]

85

```
( c = getchar ( ) ) !=EOF && c != '\n'
```

This expression is true if c is neither the EOF nor the new line character. It is essential that it is evaluated left to right, for otherwise c would have a different value for each test. Similarly, in an expression like:

```
i < limit && ( c = getchar ( ) ) != EOF && c != '\n'
```

you may want to ensure that "i < limit" is true before you read a new character. If limit specifies the maximum number of characters you can store, you want to know that the limit has not been reached before you read another character. This is guaranteed by C because evaluation proceeds from left to right and stops as soon as the truth or falsehood of the expression is known. In this example, when i<limit is false, no further evaluation of the relational expression is performed; thus no new characters are fetched.

NEGATION OPERATOR

The negation operator is denoted by the exclamation point (!). It is the NOT operator, a unary operator that reverses the truth value of its operand. For example, the expression:

```
x==5
```

is true when the value of x is five. The expression:

```
!( x==5 )
```

is false when x has the value five. The expression:

```
! found
```

is true when the value of found is zero, and false when the value of found is non-zero. The expression can be read as "not found."
The expression:

```
! (x == y)
```

is equivalent to:

```
x != y
```

In ! (x == y), the parentheses are necessary. Without the parentheses,

86

```
!x == y
```

would be evaluated as

```
(!x) == y
```

Since ! has a higher precedence than == (refer to Table 4-4), the negation operator is evaluated first in this example.

THE ?: CONDITIONAL OPERATOR

A final operator that we'll introduce in this chapter is the conditional operator ?:. ?: is a *ternary* operator. Ternary means that this operator has three operands. If you are familiar with an "if-else" statement, the ?: is sort of an "if-else" operator.

Relational expressions are often used as the first of its operand. For example, the expression:

```
a == 5 ? printf("a is 5") : printf("a is not 5")
```

is evaluated as follows:

- first, a == 5 is evaluated
- if a == 5 is true, printf("a is 5") is executed
- if a == 5 is false, printf("a is not 5")is executed.

In general, the conditional operator is written as:

```
expression-1 ? truval-expr : falseval-expr
```

Here's how the expression is evaluated:

- expression-1 is evaluated
- if expression-1 is non-zero (true), the value of the overall expression is the value of truval-expr.
- if expression-1 is zero (false), the value of the expression is the value of falseval-expr.

For example, the expression:

```
n > m ? n : m
```

has the value n if n > m is true, or the value m if n > m is false. In other words, the value of the expression is the maximum of m and n. Hence, the statement:

very efficient code!

```
max = n>m ? n : m;
```

assigns the maximum of the two variables to the variable max.
    As another example consider:

```
lowcase = ('a' <= c && c <= 'z') ? TRUE : FALSE;
```

In this statement the character variable c is tested to see if it falls
between the character constants 'a' and 'z', inclusive. If it does
(i.e., c contains a lowercase letter), the variable lowercase is
assigned the value TRUE; otherwise, it is assigned the value
FALSE. TRUE and FALSE have presumably been #defined as:

```
#define TRUE 1
#define FALSE 0
```

As one last example of the ?: operator, consider the statement:

```
nextc = stack_empty() ? getchar() : pop();
```

error should use double == to get comparison of values

This statement causes the function stack_empty() to be called. If
stack_empty() returns a non-zero value the function getchar() is
called and the value returned by getchar() is assigned to nextc. If
stack_empty() returns to zero, pop() is called and its returned
value is assigned to nextc.

PREPROCESSOR MACROS

    The use of the ?: operator to test for a lowercase character
looked like:

```
lowcase = ('a' <= c && c <= 'z') ? TRUE:FALSE;
```

Another way to write this statement is with a #define "macro." A
macro looks like a function when it's used, but it's not a
function. A #define macro for the above statement would be
defined like this:

```
#define islower(x)  ('a' <= x && x <= 'z') ? TRUE:FALSE
```

This preprocessor statement defines islower to be a macro with
one argument, shown as x. A macro is similar to a function in
that x is a formal parameter that gets replaced by the real
argument when the macro is used. It differs from a function in
that a text replacement is done by the C preprocessor, hence no
actual function call takes place.

No computation is done by the macro — computation occurs after text substitution by the preprocessor & during the

    With the islower macro in place the test can be performed
by the statement:

88

```
                    lowcase = islower(nextc);
```

The preprocessor replaces this statement with:

```
lowcase = ('a' <= nextc && nextc <= 'z') ? TRUE:FALSE;
```

When writing #define macros the following syntax rules must be observed: (a) start in column 1; (b) no spaces are allowed between the macro name and the left parenthesis starting the formal parameter list; (c) if more than one formal parameter is used to define the macro, they are separated by commas. For instance:

$$\#define \quad max(a,b) \quad (a > b \, ? \, a{:}b)$$

uses two formal parameters in its definition. When used in a program as:

```
    z = r * max(x,y);
```

the preprocessor performs the text replacement:

```
    z = r * (x > y ? x:y);
```

Because only a text replacement is being performed, care should be taken to judiciously use parentheses in the replacement text of the macro. Consider the macro:

```
#define SCALEFACTOR 100
#define scale(x)  x * SCALEFACTOR
```

Scale multiplies its argument by the **SCALEFACTOR**. If scale is used as:

```
    view = scale(r);
```

the preprocessor replaces this statement with:

```
    view = r * 100;
```

In this case everything's fine. But, if used as:

```
    view = scale(r + 1);
```

then the replacement text is:

```
    view = r + 1 * 100;
```

compilation of the source
code for the entire program

89

which was not the intent. The original intent is preserved by defining the macro as:

```
#define scale(x)  (x) * SCALEFACTOR
```

Now the replacement text will look like:

```
view = (r + 1) * 100;
```

As a general rule, macros should be liberally parenthesized to avoid possible problems. For example, a liberally parenthesized version of islower is:

```
#define islower(x)  (('a' <= (x) && (x) <= 'z') ? TRUE:FALSE)
```

EXERCISES

1. Rewrite the following statements using the operational assignment operators:

```
(a)   y = y + 1;
(b)   netpay = netpay * (1.0 + PREMIUM);
(c)   factor = factor % 10;
```

2. Given the declaration:

```
int i, z[5];
```

and the program fragment:

```
i = 1;
z[i++] = 2;
z[++i] = 3;
```

(a) to which array cell is 2 assigned?

(b) to which array cell is 3 assigned?

3. Given the declaration:

```
int i,j,k;
```

and the statements:

```
i = 5 * 2 + 3;
j = 10/2 - 3 * 4;
k = (7 % 3) + (55 % 5);
```

what values are assigned to i,j, and k?

4. Given the declarations:

```
int i = 10;   int j = 20;
```

determine which of the following relational expressions are true and which are false:

(a)   i != j

(b)   i >= j

(c)   i + 5 < j

(d)   i < 0 || i == (j - 10)

(e)   !j && !i

(f)   ! (j == i)

5. Given the declarations:

```
float r = 1.0;
float s = 0.0, z = 27.6;
```

what will the following statements print?

(a)   r == s ? printf("A") : printf("B");

(b)   z ? printf("A") : printf("B");

6. Write the following #define macros using the ?: operator:

(a) isupper   the value is TRUE if c is an uppercase letter, FALSE otherwise

(b) min(x,y)   the value is x if x is less then y, otherwise, the value is y

(c) isdigit(c)   TRUE if c is a digit, FALSE otherwise

(d) ismultiple(m,n) TRUE if m is a multiple of n (e.g., 10 is a multiple of 2 since $10 == 5 * 2$), FALSE otherwise

7. Using the sizeof operator, write a program to determine the size of int, float, char, and double on your system. Print the sizes.

Chapter 5

Loops and
Control Statements

As you have seen, C program execution begins at the first executable statement in the function main and proceeds sequentially toward the function's terminating bracket. There are times when you need to alter the program's flow to take a particular course of action depending on events. This chapter presents the statements that let you specify the order in which computation is to be performed.

In this chapter we'll use flowcharts to indicate the program flow that results from using a particular control statement. The flowcharts will mostly be composed of boxes and diamonds. Boxes represent actions being performed and diamonds represent decision points. Interconnecting lines and arrows will show the resulting program flow. As an example, Fig. 5-1 shows the type of illustrations that will be used. The program flow the figure starts by making a decision regarding the value of x. The labeled arrows show that if x has a non zero value the program flow goes to statement 1; if the value of x is zero, program flow goes to statement 2.

THE IF STATEMENT

The If statement is used to test a condition and then execute statements depending on the outcome of the test. In its simplest form the syntax of the If statement is:

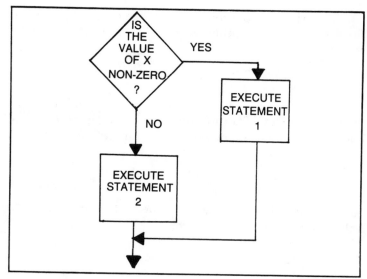

Fig. 5-1. Sample Flowchart.

```
if( expression )
    statement-1;

next-sequential-statement;
```

In this form, expression is evaluated. If its value is non zero statement 1 is executed, then control passes to the next sequential statement. If expression has a value of zero then statement 1 is not executed, but control passes directly to the next sequential statement.

We have drawn a box around the complete If statement in our flowchart. Syntactically, the boxed-in portion is one statement. We'll draw similar boxes around control statements throughout this chapter.

Recall from the discussion of relational operators that when a relational expression is false its value is zero. Similarly, a true relational expression has a value of one. Hence, you can use relational expressions in an If statement, as in the following example:

```
y = 0;
if ( x >= 10)
        y = big(x);
printf("%d",y);
```

In this example the function big is called only when the text x >= 10 is true. In this event, the value of the relational expression is non zero. The statement calling big is indented to indicate that its execution is conditional on the If statement.

The expression portion of the If statement does not have to involve relational operators. For instance, the program fragment:

```
if(found)
      y=foundit();
```

is perfectly legal C. The function foundit is called if the value of the variable found is non zero. The program fragment:

```
if(checkstat())
      error();
```

causes the function checkstat to be called. If it returns a non zero value the function error is called.

In the statement:

```
if( x = y * 3.5)
            printf("%f %f", x, y);
```

y is multiplied by 3.5 and the result is assigned to x. Note that the single equal sign is an assignment, not a test for equality. If the value assigned to x is non zero, printf is called. This is perfectly legal in C and can cause problems for the uninitiated who might think it means:

```
if(x == y * 3.5)
      printf("%f %f", x,y);
```

This program fragment compares the value of x to the result of y times 3.5. If the two values are equal, printf is called.

Figure 5-2 depicts the syntax and a flowchart of the statement.

COMPOUND STATEMENTS

Statement 1 of the syntax definition can be a *compound statement*. A compound statement is a group of one or more statements enclosed in braces. When using a compound statement as part of the If statement, the result looks like this:

```
if ( expression ) {
      statement-1a;
      statement-1b;
      statement-1c;
            .
            .
            .
}

next-sequential-statement;
```

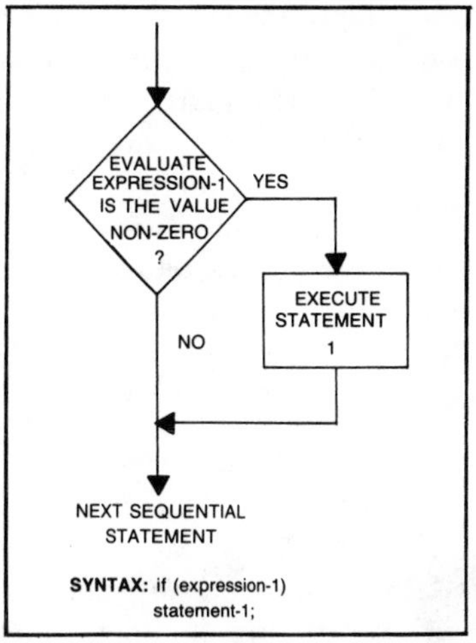

Fig. 5-2. The flowchart
and syntax of the If statement.

In this form the statements within the braces (1a, 1b, etc.) form
a compound statement and they are all executed when the
expression is non zero. When the expression is zero they are all
skipped.

Again, note that the boxed-in portion is syntactically one C
statement. Also notice that there is no semicolon after the
terminating brace of the compound statement.

When using the If statement it is important to indent the
source code in such a way that a reader can tell how the program
flows. The style of indentation used here is indicated by the
compound statement following the if above. There the bracket
beginning the compound statement is on the same line as "if
(expression)", and the brace closing the compound statement
is indented to the same level as the if.

Another style is:

```
if(expression)
    (
    statement-1a;
    statement-1b;
        .
        .
        .
    )
```

Generally, the former style is easy to read and easy to edit using
text editors. In your own programs use a style that's clear to you.

When a compound statement is introduced it is permissable
to declare new variables within the compound statement. The
scope of these variables is the duration of the compound

statement. For example, you consider the code shown in Listing 5-1. Within the compound statement following the if, a new variable i is declared and is local to the compound statement. This variable i is different from the i declared outside the compound statement. When this new i is assigned the value five in the compound statement the assignment has no effect on the other variable i. Hence, this little program prints two lines that look like:

```
In the if statement i = 5 and j = 1
Outside of the if statement i = 0 and j = 1
```

The compound statement is still part of the main function, so all the variables that can be referenced by main can be referenced in the compound statement. But, whenever a name is redeclared in a compound statement (such as we did with i) the most recent declaration prevails.

The capability to declare new variables in compound statements is not supported by all microcomputer C compilers. Check your compiler's specifications before attempting this.

Listing 5-1. Introducing new variables in compound statements.

```
#include <stdio.h>

main() {

        int i,j;

        i = 0;
        j = 1;
        if(i == 0) {
                int i;

                i = 5;
                printf("\tIn the if statement ");
                printf("i = %d and j = %d \n", i, j);

        }
        printf("Outside of the if statement ");
        printf("i = %d and j = %d \n", i,j);
```

IF-ELSE STATEMENT

An optional *Else* can be used as part of the If statement resulting in the syntax:

```
if(expression)
      statement-1;
else
      statement-2;

next-sequential-statement;
```

In the case, if the value of the expression is nonzero, statement 1 is executed and statement 2 is skipped; while if the value of expression is zero, statement 1 is skipped and statement 2 is executed. Either statement 1 or statement 2 (or both) can be compound statements. As an example:

```
if(number > 100)
      printf("number is greater than 100");
else
      printf("number is not greater than 100");
```

As another example, remember the function upper in Chapter 4 which converted the lowercase letter to uppercase? Here is a version, using If-Else, that makes sure its argument is indeed a lowercase letter (see Listing 5-2). Figure 5-3 depicts the program flow of the If-Else statement.

Statement 2 in the If-Else statement can also be another if statement. In this way, If-Else statements can be chained together:

```
if(expression-1)
      statement-1;
else if(expression-2)
      statement-2;
else if(expression-3)
      statement-3;
             .
             .
else if (expression-n)
      statement-n;
else
      statement-(n+1);

next-sequential-statement;
```

but you can end either here or) *here*

last statement in chain does NOT contain the "If"

Here the expressions are evaluated in order (expression-1, expression-2, etc). The first true (non zero) expression causes the corresponding statement to be executed and the entire chain to be broken (control will pass to the next sequential statement following the chain of ifs). For instance, if expression-1 == 0, expression-2 == 0, and expression-3 == 5, then statement-3 is executed and no further expressions are evaluated.

which it also should be noted does NOT contain an "if"

If all the expressions are false (zero) the last statement (n+1) is executed. This serves as a default or "none-of-the-above" statement. Its use is optional, so the last else and statement-(n+1) need not be present. In this case, if each of expression-1 through expression-n has a zero value none of the corresponding statements is executed.

Fig. 5-4 graphically depicts this construction. As before,

any (or all) of the statements can be compound statements. This construction is often called a *multiway branch* and the figure shows that it allows control to branch off in one of several directions.

Listing 5-2. An example of an If-Else statement.

```
to_upper(letter) char letter; {
        /* convert lower case ASCII letters to upper case */

        if ( 'a' <= letter && letter <= 'z' )
                /* yes it is lower case, convert it */
                return(letter - 32);
        else
                /* no it is not lower case, leave it alone */
                return(letter);
}
```

NESTED IF-ELSE STATEMENTS

The If-Else statement can be nested, as in:

```
if(expression-1)
        if(expression-2)
                statement-a;
        else
                statement-b;
else
        statement-c;
next-sequential-statement;
```

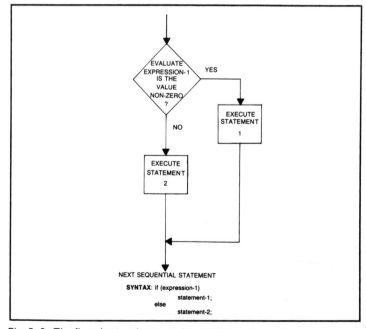

Fig. 5-3. The flowchart and syntax of the If-Else statement.

98

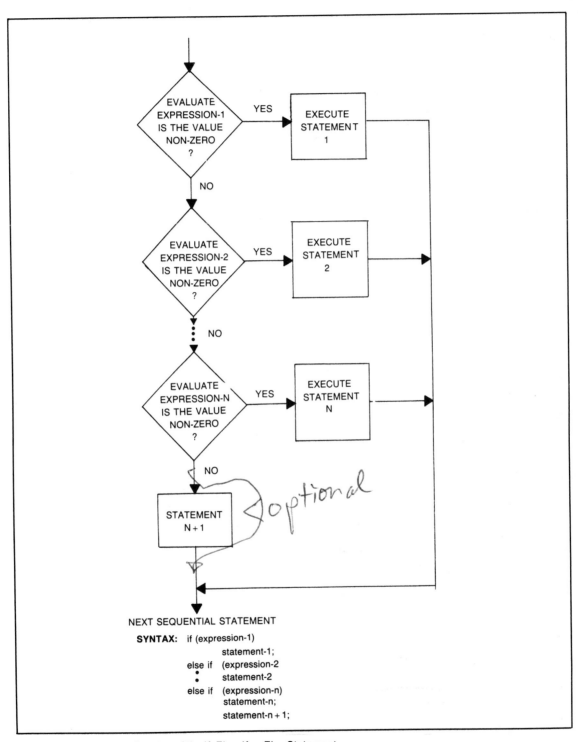

Fig. 5-4. A flowchart and syntax of the If–Else–If . . . Else Statement.

Table 5-1 shows how the statements are executed for given values of expression-1 and expression-2. Because the entire if–else statement is syntactically one statement, no braces are necessary in our above example.

As another example of nested ifs, Listing 5–3 characterizes an input character. Try running this program on your system.

Table 5–1 Example of Nested If Evaluation.

Value of Expression-1	Value of Expression-2	Statement Executed
nonzero	nonzero	statement-a
nonzero	zero	statement-b
zero	not evaluated	statement-c

Listing 5–3. Example of nested ifs.

```
#include <stdio.h>

#define TRUE 1
#define FALSE 0
#define SPACE ' '        * octal number
#define DEL '\0177'                /* The ASCII DEL character */

/* Define some preprocessor macros (See Chapter 4) to help
   characterize characters  */

#define islower(c)  'a' <= (c)  &&  (c) <= 'z' ? TRUE : FALSE
#define isupper(c)  'A' <= (c)  &&  (c) <= 'Z' ? TRUE : FALSE
#define isdigit(c)  '0' <= (c)  &&  (c) <= '9' ? TRUE : FALSE
#define printable(c)  SPACE  <= (c)  &&  (c) <= DEL ? TRUE : FALSE

whatis(c)  char c; {
        if( printable(c) )
                if( islower(c) )
                        printf( " a lower case letter\n");
                else if ( isupper(c) )
                        printf(" an upper case letter\n");
                else if ( isdigit(c) )
                        printf(" a digit\n");
                else if ( c == '\t' || c == '\n' || c == SPACE )
                        printf(" white space\n");
                else
                        printf(" punctuation or a special symbol");
        else
                printf(" a nonprintable character\n");

}

main() {
        char achar;
        printf("Type any character .... then carriage return\n");
        achar = getchar();    <--- echo to screen what was typed
        putchar('\n');
        printf("The character you typed is");
        whatis(achar);

}
```

Care must be taken when nesting ifs when some of the If statements do not use the optional Else. For example, in the program fragment:

```
if( x>y )
    if ( c != 0 )
        printf("x is greater than y and c is nonzero\n");
    else
        printf("x is greater than y and c is zero\n");
```

the else is associated with the most previous *if* statement that doesn't already have an Else. The Else above associates with the If (c ! = 0) condition as the indentation indicates. This association of Elses can be altered by using braces to force a different association. For instance:

```
if(x > y ) {
    if(c !=0 )
        printf("x is greater than y. c is nonzero\n");
}
else
        printf("x is less than or equal to y\n");
```

Here use of braces forces the Else to associate with the "if(x>y)" test.

In these examples the use of tests such as if (c ! = 0) can be shortened to appear as if(c). Since C defines the truth of an expression as a nonzero value, if(c) is exactly equivalent to if(c ! = 0). Similarly, a test such as if (flag == 0) can be written as if(!flag). You should use the version that makes the program most readable.

WHILE LOOPS

The purpose of a loop is to repeatedly execute indicated program statements. Loops can be thought of as having two components: loop control and a loop body. The *loop body* is the set of program statements to be repeatedly executed. *Loop control* determines when and if the loop body will be executed.

The while loop is a mechanism to repeatedly execute a statement (compound or simple) as long as an expression is true (nonzero). The syntax of the while loop is:

```
while (expression)
    statement-1;

next-sequential-statement;
```

When statement-1 is a compound statement, the loop appears as:

```
while(expression) {
        statement-1a;
        statement-1b;
        statement-1c;

              .
              .
              .

}

next-sequential-statement;
```

The parenthesized expression is the loop control expression.

The while loop operates as follows: first the expression is evaluated. If it is nonzero, statement-1 is executed and the expression is evaluated again. If it is still nonzero, statement-1 is reexecuted and the expression is reevaluated. This looping continues until the expression has a value of zero. At this point control skips past statement-1 to the next sequential statement. This operation implies that if the expression has a zero value upon the entry to the loop (i.e., the first time the expression is evaluated), statement-1 is never executed.

Figure 5-5 presents a flowchart of the while loop.

Listing 5-4 illustrates the use of while loops. In the function fill array, the while loop is used to repeatedly execute the statements which fill array cells with characters. In print array the while loop is used to print the array cells. Note that the loop body of each while loop is a compound statement enclosed in braces.

As another example of a while loop, consider the function echo in Listing 5-5. The while loop in echo reads a character, stores it in the variable c, and checks to see if EOF was read. If EOF was not read, the relational expression is true, so the statement putchar(c) is executed. The next character is then read, stored and checked against EOF. When EOF is read the relational expression is false so its value is zero. This terminates the loop and terminates the function. Note that EOF is not written to the output string.

Echo illustrates another aspect of C worth noting. It is not unusual for loop control expressions to do a lot of work in C programs. In echo, the loop control expression performs the input, the storing of the input character, and the check for end of file. Expressions like:

```
( (c=getchar()) != EOF)
```

are common in C and you will get used to them as you write

Handwritten margin notes:

1. get input from keyboard or file
2. store input in variable c
3. compare input with EOF (which is null character)
4. set value of entire expression equal to "1" if input is NOT EOF or "0" if input is EOF

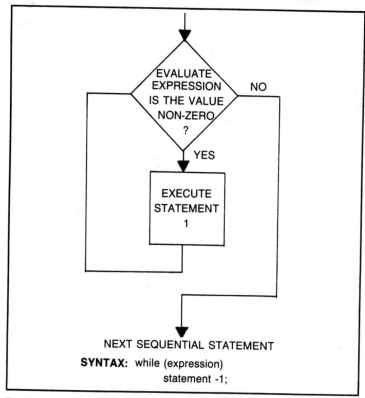

EVALUATE
EXPRESSION
IS THE VALUE
NON-ZERO
?

NO

YES

EXECUTE
STATEMENT
1

NEXT SEQUENTIAL STATEMENT

SYNTAX: while (expression)
    statement -1;

Fig. 5-5. A flowchart and syntax of the while statement.

more C programs. With a more restrictive definition of what loop control expressions could be (say, only relational expressions), a simple function like echo would take more lines of code to express. As an example of this, consider the version of echo in Listing 5-6. In this version of echo, we have restricted the control expressions of the while loop and the if statement to be relational expressions only. You can see that several more lines of code were required to express the same logic. The generality of the control expression in the C loops and control statements can be effectively used to make program logic compact yet clear. This will be seen again in our discussion of the for loop in the next section.

For completeness, let's write a main function to use echo. In Listing 5-7, the first version of echo is used. How useful is this simple program? Recall from the discussion of redirecting standard I/O (Chapter 1) that getchar and putchar are reading and writing the standard input and output, respectively. Hence, this program can be used to copy one file to another, list a file on the screen, print a file to the printer, etc. Just by redirecting the standard I/O at run time, you can make echo quite versatile. In

Listing 5-4. Examples of while loops.

[handwritten annotations: "define i as an integer", "define letter as an array variable with size of 15", "define a function called fill array", "set i to zero", "printf do linefeed", "call input & assign it to letters[i] variable", "increment i"]

```
                #include <stdio.h>

                char letters[15];
                int i;

                fill_array() {

                        i = 0;
                        printf("Enter 15 letters, then carriage return\n");
                        while(i < 15)  {
                                letters[i] = getchar();
                                i++;
                        }
                }

                print_array() {

                        i = 0;
                        printf("The letters you entered were\n");
                        while(i < 15)  {
                                printf("%c",letters[i]);
                                i++;
                        }
                }

                main() {

                        fill_array();
                        print_array();

                }
```

fact, if your system supports I/O redirection, try using this program to copy one file into another.

As another example of the while loop, consider the function strlen in Listing 5-8, which computes the length of a string. The while loop's control expression is simply stated as "s[len]"—an element of the array s. Since s represents a string, we know it will be terminated by an end-of-string marker ($'\0'$), which has the value zero. Thus, this while loop will

Listing 5-5. Function echo, version one.

```
                #include <stdio.h>

                echo() {  /* echo the input stream to the output */

                        int c;
                        while( (c = getchar() ) != EOF )
                                putchar(c);
                }
```

Listing 5-6. Echo function, version two.

```
#define TRUE  1
#define FALSE  0

echo() {
        int c;
        int moreinput;

        moreinput = TRUE;
        while(moreinput == TRUE) {
                c = getchar();
                if(c == EOF)
                        moreinput = FALSE;
                else
                        putchar(c);
        }
}
```

marker

execute until the end-of-string maker is detected. Equivalently, we could have written:

```
while(s[len] != '\0')
```

However, the former style is very common in C and you should be aware of its use. *marker*

When the end-of-string maker is reached the while loop immediately ceases to iterate. Consequently, the end-of-string marker is not counted. This is as it should be; the end-of-string marker is a *marker*, not a character of the string. However, this implies that strlen(s)+1 characters are actually required to store the string s.

Listing 5-7. Main function using echo.

```
#include <stdio.h>

echo() {  /* echo the input stream to the output */

        int c;
        while( (c = getchar() ) != EOF )
                putchar(c);
}

main() {
        echo();

}
```

FOR LOOPS — *For Next Step*

For loops are another mechanism to repeatedly execute program statements. In contrast to the while loop, the for loop

Listing 5-8. The function strlen.

```
strlen(s) char s[];   { /* Compute the number of
                          characters in the array s */
        int len;

        len = 0;
        while(s[len])
                len++;

        return(len);

    }
```

this calls up the value of the variable s[len]. If the variable is not 0 then len is incremented. If it is zero then the end of the file EOF has been reached of the value of the expression is False (i.e. equal to zero) and the while loop is terminated without incrementing len.

has three loop control expressions. The syntax of the for loop is:

```
for(init-expr; test-expr; increment-expr)
    statement-1;

next-sequential-statement;
```

The three loop control expressions are named in a way that is suggestive of how they often used. Init-expr is an expression that is evaluated only once. It is evaluated first and it often serves to initialize some variables that will be used within the loop. Test-expr is the expression whose non zero value will cause statement-1 to be executed and whose zero value will cause control to skip past statement-1 to the next sequential statement. Increment-expr is an expression that is evaluated after each execution of statement-1. It is often used for incrementing loop control variables.

Operation of the for loop is as follows:

- Evaluate init-expr
- Evaluate test-expr
- If test-expr has a zero value exit the for loop
- If test-expr has a non zero value execute statement-1, evaluate the increment-expr, go back to step 2.

Figure 5-6 presents a flowchart of the for statement's operation. As a simple example, consider a for loop which increments a counter 100 times:

```
for( i = 0; i < 100 ; i++ )
    counter++ ;
```

It performs the same looping function as the BASIC statements:

```
30 FOR I = 0 TO 99
40 COUNTER = COUNTER + 1
50 NEXT I
```

106

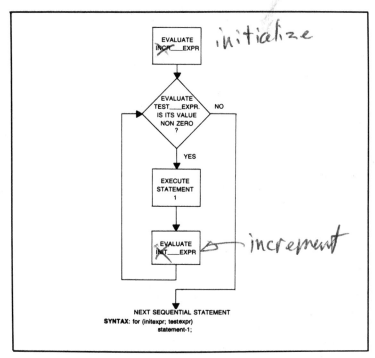

initialize

increment

Fig. 5-6. A flowchart and syntax of the for loop.

To clarify things, consider the function put in Listing 5-9. Here, you see a straightforward application of the for loop. The init-expr (i = 0) initializes a variable used to index the array. This is done only once, at the beginning of the loop. The test-expr (s[i] ! = '\0') looks for the end-of-string marker. When the end-of-string marker is not present (i.e., s[i] ! = '\0' is true), putchar writes s[i] to the output. The increment-expr (i++) increments i to index the next element of the array s. When the end-of-string marker is found (i.e., s[i] ! = '\0' is false) the loop terminates and the function returns.

As another example, consider the function countchar, which will count the number of occurrences of a specified character in a string (Listing 5-10). The for loop of countchar processes the character array just as the loop in puts did.

Notice that the body of the for loop (the If statement) is not enclosed in braces as are compound statements. Syntactically the "if(expr) statement-1;" is considered to be one statement and the braces are not necessary. Similarly, "while(expr) statement;", and "for(. . .) statement;" are syntactically one statement.

The same function can be written with a while loop, as in Listing 5-11.

107

Listing 5-9. A for loop example.

```
puts(s) char s[]; {
        /* write the string s to the standard output */

        int i;

        for(i=0; s[i] != '\0'; i++)
                putchar(s[i]);
}
```

You can quickly write a program to test countchar to gain some confidence that it will work (see Listing 5-12). When compiled and run, the program or Listing 5-12 prints:

```
The variable i was assigned 3
The variable j was assigned 5
```

where 3 and 5 are the number of "t's" in each of the strings.

Note the two different methods of passing information to countchar that have been employed. The first call passes the name of an external character array (test) and an external character (c); both were initialized outside the function main. The second call passes a literal string ("yet another test string") and a literal character ('t'). These literals are appropriately quoted to indicate that they are what they are (a string and a character constant) and not variable names.

The while loop version of countchar is indicative of a more general situation. Namely, the loop:

```
for (init-expr; test-expr; increment-expr)
    statement-1;
```

Listing 5-10. The function countchar, with a for loop.

name of function is countchar & it must be passed two variables

```
countchar(x,c) char x[], c; {
        /* count the number of occurences of the character
           c in the string x */
        int i, count;

        count = 0;
        for(i = 0; x[i] != '\0'; i++)
                if(x[i] == c)
                        count++;
        return(count);
}
```

both variables x[] & c are of the type characters the first is a string which means a series of characters

define both i & count as integer variables

this statement is executed only once at the end of the function after the for loop has been completed. It assigns the value of count as the value of the function

108

Listing 5-11. The function countchar with a while loop.

```
countchar(x,c) char x[], c;   {

        int i, count;

        count = 0;
        i = 0;
        while(x[i] != '\0')   {
                if(x[i] == c)
                        count++;
                i++;
        }

        return(count);

}
```

is equivalent to the code:

```
init-expr;
while (test-expr) {
      statement-1;
      increment-expr;
}
```

The use of a for loop versus a while loop is usually a matter of style. Since in countchar, the variable i was used to march across the array x[], it makes sense to show this as a loop control variable as the for loop does.

Getline

In Exercise 4 of Chapter 1 you determined whether a function called getline is available on your system. Usually this

Listing 5-12. Testing countchar.

```
#include <stdio.h>
char test[] = "string for testing";
char c = 't';

        main()   {

                int i;
                int j;

                i = countchar(test,c);
                j = countchar("yet another test string",'t');

                printf("The variable i was assigned %d\n",i);
                printf("The variable j was assigned %d\n",j);

        }
```

both c & 't' are testing for the presence of the letter t

function is supplied by the compiler manufacturer and is automatically linked into programs that use it. In the event that getline is not available on your system, a version of the function is presented in Listing 5-13. It illustrates the use of the for loop.

In the for statement the text-expr in is pretty long. We first check that i<=max-2 is true. This check ensures that at least two array cells (line[max −2] and line[max −1]) are still vacant—one for the next character, and one for the end-of-string marker. Since the relational expression:

```
i<=max-2 && (c=getchar()) !=EOF && c !=EOL
```

is evaluated from left to right, you know that space is available in the array before getchar is called. Under normal circumstances, the for loop terminates when either EOF or EOL is returned by getchar.

The getline function presented here behaves in the standard manner: the line read by getline is terminated with an end-of-string marker, the new line character (EOL) is included in the line, and a count of the number of characters read is returned to the caller. The count includes the EOL character but does not include the end-of-string marker.

Listing 5-13. A version of the function getchar.

```
#define  EOL    '\n'     /*  The end-of-line character */


getline(line, max)
        char line[];
        int max;

{

        /* Get a line of input and store it in array line[].  Max is the
        maximum number of characters that the array can hold.  Terminate
        the line with a C end-of-string marker.  Return the number of
        characters read */

        int i,c;

        for(i = 0; i <= max-2) && (c = getchar() ) != EOF && c != EOL; i++)
                line[i] = c;

        /* If the last character read was the end-of-line character,
           save it */
        if(c == EOL)
                line[i++] = c;

        /* terminate the line with the end-of-string mark '\0' */
        line[i] = '\0';
        return(i);

}
```

Note that with the declarations:

```
int n;
char input[80];
```

a call to getline of the form:

```
n = getline(input, 80);
```

will read at most 79 characters (including the new line character). One position in the array is reserved for the end-of string marker. Also note that you can determine if the line was too long to fit into the array. For the above declarations, the program fragment:

```
n = getline(input, 80);
if( n == 79 && input[78] != EOL )
    /* the input line was too long */
```

illustrates how an input overflow can be detected.

This version of getline may require minor modification to work correctly on your system. Namely, the preprocessor statement

```
#define EOL '\n'
```

may need to be changed. EOL must match the value produced when you strike the carriage return key. An alternative definition might be:

```
#define EOL '\r'
```

The correct value depends on the compiler you are using.

In the remainder of this text, several programs use getline. If getline was not supplied with your compiler, be sure to complete Exercise 5 at the end of this chapter.

Null Statements

An often-used feature of C loops is to make the statement that constitutes the body of the loop (what we have been calling "statement-1") be the null statement. The null statement is a semicolon by itself. Syntactically it's a statement, but it doesn't perform any operations. For instance, consider a for loop version of strlen, the function that was previously written with a while loop (Listing 5-14). The loop control expressions of the for loop are doing all the work. The variable len is initialized to zero and used both as the array index and the counter to count

111

Listing 5-14. For-loop version of strlen.

```
strlen(s) char s[]; (
        int len;
        for(len = 0; s[len] != '\0'; len++)
                ;
        return(len);

)
```

the characters. The loop body is a null statement. The fact that
the value of len is returned illustrates another important aspect
of C for loops: the loop control variables retain their values after
the loop completes. The value returned by strlen is the value of
len that made the test "s[len] ! ='\0'" false (verify for yourself
that this correctly counts the number of characters in the string).
Further, it is permissible to alter the value of loop control
variables within the loop body.

When null statements are used it is good practice (but
certainly not required) to put the semicolon on a line by itself.
Strlen could have been written as shown in Listing 5-15. Here
the body of the for loop is the null statement and the semicolon
is on the same line as the loop control information. In this style
the semicolon tends to get lost. Of course the lack of indentation
provides a clue to what is being expressed, but the former style is
better. However, watch out for the latter style when you read C
programs written by other people; it is frequently used.

Omitting Loop Control Expressions

It is permissible in the for loop to leave out any (or all) of
the loop control expressions. When this is done semicolons
must still be used to indicate that something was left out. If init-
expression is left out no initialization is performed, but
otherwise the loop behavior is the same. This case has the
syntax:

```
for( ; test-expr; increment-expr)
     statement-1;
```

Listing 5-15. Another version of strlen.

```
strlen(s) char s[]; (
        int len;
        for(len = 0; s[len] != '\0'; len++);
        return(len);

)
```

For example, consider the for loop in the function power (Listing 5–16). The for loop control variable (n) did not require initialization so no init-expr is used in the for loop. Recall that when a function definition begins:

```
double power (x,n)
```

it means that power will return a result of type double.

In a similar fashion, if the increment-expr is left out loop behavior remains the same except there is no increment-expr to evaluate after statement-1 is executed. Syntactically, it is written like this:

```
for(init-expr; test-expr;   )
        statement-1;
```

When both init-expr and increment-expr are left out, the syntax appears as:

```
for ( ; test-expr; )
        statement-1;
```

Listing 5–16. The function power.

```
double power(x,n)
        double x;
        int n;
                {

        /* raise x to to the nth power.  If n == 0, the result is 1.  If n
           is negative, the result is 1.0/(x to the -n power)  */

        double result;
        int negpower;

        if(n == 0)
                return(1.0);

        negpower = 1;
        if(n < 0)   {
                negpower = -1;   /* remember negative exponent */
                n = -n;          /* make n positive */
        }

        result = 1.0;
        for(; n; n--)
                result *= x;
        return( negpower > 0 ? result : 1.0/result );

        }
```

The behavior of the loop in this case is identical to:

```
while(test-expr)
     statement-1;
```

Finally, if test-expr is left out the loop's test condition is considered to always be true. Hence:

```
for(init-expr; ; increment-expr)
     statement-1;
```

causes a loop that will indefinitely execute statement-1. Unless that is what you want (i.e., an infinite loop), statement-1 must in some way cause the looping to cease. There are a couple of ways this can be done. Statement-1 might be a compound statement with a return embedded in the infinite loop. If the loop is inside a function, the return will cause it to cease executing. Or the loop might contain a break statement—a statement we'll discuss shortly.

Loops that execute until some condition within the loop terminates them are sometimes useful. In fact, a mechanism employed by some C programmers is to use the following #define statement:

```
#define forever    for(;;)
```

An example of when this construct might be used is a program that continuously monitors an alarm system. Such a program might look like Listing 5-17. The for loop in this example will execute "forever".

Comma Operator

The comma operator (,) is used to specify left to right evaluation of expressions in a statement. For example, in:

```
x = 0, y = 2;
```

two expressions are separated by the comma operator. They are evaluated left to right so the assignment to x takes place first, then the assignment to y. The type and value of expressions separated by the comma operator is the type and value of the last expression evaluated. The comma operator has the lowest precedence of all C operators.

The comma operator is most often seen in for statements. For example, in:

Listing 5-17. Example using an infinite for loop.

```
#define forever for(;;)
#define ON 1

main()  {
        int status;

        /* initialize sensors */
        initsensors();

        /* start monitoring alarms */

        forever  {

                status = alarmsys1();
                if(status == ON)
                        phonepolice();

                status = alarmsys2();
                if(status == ON )
                        signalfire();

        }

}
```

```
for(i=0,j=1; condition; i++,j++){
        .
        .
        .

        loop statements

}
```

the comma operator is used in both the init-expr (i=0, j=1;) and the increment-expr (i++, j++). In this way two variables can be initialized and incremented as part of the loop control. The function "index" illustrates this use. Index has two arguments; each is a character string. It determines if one string is contained in the other (see Listing 5-18).

You can run program Listing 5-19 to test index. In this program getline is used to read input lines. If getline is not available on your system make sure the version presented earlier is stored on disk (see Exercise 5). Listing 5-19A is sample output from running the program.

As another example of the comma operator, consider a program that will repeatedly prompt a user for data then read and process the result. We'll use getline to read the data. Assume the function "process" actually processes the data. One way to write such a program is shown in Listing 5-20. The statement

Listing 5-18. The function index.

```
index(s,t)  char s[],t[];  {

        /* Find out if t is a substring of s.  If it is, return the index
           of where t begins in s.  If it's not, return -1 */

        int i,j,k;

        /* Start marching across the string s*/

        for(i = 0; s[i] != '\0'; i++)  {
                /* See if t[] matches the string s[i],s[i+1],... */
                for(j = i, k = 0; t[k] == s[j] && t[k] != '\0'; j++, k++)
                                        ;

                if(t[k] == '\0')
                        /* t[] matched when we started with s[i] */
                        return(i);

        }
        /* We've reached the end of s without finding t*/
                return(-1);
}
```

"printf("Enter Data>")" appears twice—outside the while loop so it is executed before the first call to getline, and inside the while loop so it is executed before each subsequent call to getline.

Using the comma operator, the function can be written as shown in Listing 5-21. The comma separated expressions inside while parentheses perform both the prompt for the data and the call to getline to read the data.

The comma operator's left-to-right execution guarantees the prompt will come before the data is read. Since the value of comma separated expressions is the value of the last expression evaluated, the loop will continue until getline returns zero.

BREAK STATEMENT

The break statement is a statement that can be used within a loop or a switch (to be discussed). A break statement causes a loop to terminate immediately. When the break is executed control immediately passes to the statement following the loop. The dotted line in Fig. 5-6 shows how a break statement affects a for loop.

To illustrate the use of a break statement in a loop we'll write a function called getword. We'll define a word to be any string of contiguous characters (except space, tab, or newline). In the string:

```
"This is\t a word string\n"
```

Listing 5-19. A test of index.

```
#include <stdio.h>

/* If getline is not available on your system
   uncomment the following #include statement

#include "getline.c"

*/



index(s,t)  char s[], t[];  {
        int i,j,k;
        for(i = 0; s[i] != '\0'; i++)  {
                for(j = i, k = 0; t[k] == s[j] && t[k] != '\0'; j++, k++)
                                                                   ;
                if(t[k] == '\0')
                        return(i);

        }
        return(-1);

}

main()  {
        char string[81], substring[81];
        int i,m,n,j;

        for(i = 0; i < 5; i++)  {
                printf("\nEnter a string...then carriage return\n");
                m = getline(string, 81);
                printf("\nEnter 2nd string...carriage return\n");
                n = getline(substring, 81);

                /* Get rid of the newline characters saved by saved by getline */
                string[m-1] = '\0';
                substring[n-1] = '\0';

                printf("\n");
                printf("\n%s\n", substring);
                if( (j = index(string, substring) ) < 0 )
                        printf("is not contained in\n");
                else
                        printf("starts at position %d in\n", j);
                printf("%s\n", string);

        }

}
```

Listing 5-19A. Sample output, from program 5-19.

```
                    Enter a string...then carriage return
                    this is a test
                    Enter 2nd string...carriage return
                    test

                    test
                    starts at position 10 in
                    this is a test



                    Enter a string...then carriage return
                    hello everybody
                    Enter 2nd string...carriage return
                    hello

                    hello
                    starts at position 0 in
                    hello everybody



                    Enter a string...then carriage return
                    hello everybody
                    Enter 2nd string...carriage return
                    HELLO

                    HELLO
                    is not contained in
                    hello everybody



                    Enter a string...then carriage return
                    another test string
                    Enter 2nd string...carriage return
                    ing

                    ing
                    starts at position 16 in
                    another test string



                    Enter a string...then carriage return
                    today is the first day
                    Enter 2nd string...carriage return
                    day 1


                    day 1
                    is not contained in
                    today is the first day
```

Listing 5-20. A query and response example.

```
#include <stdio.h>

/*  If you need our version of getline, be sure to include
    it here :

#include "getline.c"
*/

#define BUFSIZE 100
main() {
        char buffer[BUFSIZE];

        printf("Enter data>");
        while(  getline(buffer, BUFSIZE)  )  {
                process(buffer);
                printf("Enter data>");

        }

}

process(buffer)  char buffer[]; {
        printf("\nSimulated processing of the text:\n");
        printf("%s\n", buffer);
}
```

Listing 5-21. A query and response example using the comma operator.

```
#include <stdio.h>

/*  If necessary, include getline here

#include "getline.c"
*/

#define BUFSIZE 100

main()  {
        char buffer[BUFSIZE];

        while(printf("Enter data>"), getline(buffer, BUFSIZE) )
                process(buffer);

}


process(buffer) char buffer[];
{
        printf("\nSimulated processing of the line:\n");
        printf("%s\n", buffer);
}
```

(where \t and \n are the C escapes for tab, and newline), there are five words:

```
This
is
a
word
string
```

Here's getword (Listing 5-22). The If statement in the for loop checks to see if a word separator has been read. If so the for loop is broken with a break statement. If not the character is saved and the loop continues to iterate. The If statement (and the break) can be eliminated by putting the test for the white space into the test-expr of the for loop. In this case the for loop looks like this:

```
for(i=1; i<limit-1 && (c=getchar())!=EOF
      && !(c==' '||c=='\t'|| c=='\n');i++)
          word [i]=c;
```

Listing 5-22. The function getwork.

```
#define EOL   '\n'       /*  EOL represents the end-of-line character.
                          See the discussion at the end of the section
                          "Getline"  */

getword(word, limit)
        char word[];     /* buffer to store the word */
        int limit;       /* max number of characters that word[] can hold */

        {
        int i,c;

        /* skip leading white space */

        while( (c = getchar() ) == ' ' || c == '\t' || c == EOL )
                            ;
        if(c == EOF)  {
                word[0] = '\0';    /* makes word[] empty */
                return(0);
        }

        word[0] = c;

        for(i = 1; i < limit-1 && (c = getchar() ) != EOF; i++)
                if(c == ' ' || c == '\t' || c == EOL )
                        break;
                else
                        word[i] = c;

        word[i] = '\0';  /* terminate string */

        return(i);

}
```

This approach makes the test expr of the for statement more complex. The version with the break is easier to understand.

In Exercise 5 you will test the getword function, tailoring it to your system. Save the function in a file called "getword.c" because we will use it later.

When loops are nested the break causes the innermost loop (or switch) to be broken. In:

```
for(...){
        while(...) {
                .

                .

                .

                break;
        }
}
```

the break statement shown causes the while loop to terminate but the for loop continues on its merry way. Break statements can be used in for, while, and do-while loops, and in the switch statement. Switch and do-while have not been discussed but will be shortly.

CONTINUE STATEMENT

Since you have just finished examining the break statement you can easily learn a similar statement—continue. The continue statement can be used inside a loop to cause the loop to go immediately to its next iteration. Continue can be used in the for, while, and do-while loops.

An example of continue is a function which we'll call *nospace*. Nospace counts all the characters in a string except spaces (see Listing 5-23).

Listing 5-23. The function nospace.

```
nospace(string)  char string[];  {

        int i, count;
        for(count = 0, i = 0; string[i] != '\0'; i++)  {
                if(string[i] == ' ' )
                        continue;

                count++;

        }
        return(count);

}
```

In the body of this function, when string[i] has a space, the "continue" statement is executed. This causes the increment-expr (i++) of the for statement to be evaluated, then the for statement's test expr is evaluated. Of course when this happens, the count++ statement is not executed.

It's easy to rewrite this function without the continue statement. You merely need to reverse the sense of the test. The for loop then looks like this:

```
for(count=0,i=0; string[i]!='\0'; i++)
    if(string[i]!= ' ') /*reversed test*/
        count++;
```

The principle difference between this implementation and the one with the continue statement, is that now the count++ statement is nested one additional level. Hence, if the count++ statement was actually a compound statement (perhaps with more nesting of its own), the use of the continue statement can reduce the depth of nesting within the program.

SWITCH

The switch statement is a control statement that lets the program effect a multiway branch. You've seen one way to perform multiway branching—the chained use of If-Else-If...else. Consider the following implementation of a multiway branch where a different variable is incremented depending on the value of a variable k:

```
if(k==4)
    four++;
else if(k==5)
    five++;
else if(k==6||k==7)
    sixorsev++;
else
    other++;
```

In this case the test in each If statement is comparing k to a constant. When only constants are involved in the comparison the switch statement can be used to provide the same type of multiway branching. For example, the same result as above can be achieved using the switch statement as follows:

```
switch(k) {

    case 4:
        four++;
        break;
```

```
case 5:
        five++;
        break;

case 6:
case 7:
        sixorsev++;
        break;

    default:
            other++;
            break;

};
```

Keyword

Each constant to which the value of k is compared is labeled
with the keyboard case and followed by a colon. These constants
must have different values for each case. If k matches that case
the corresponding statements are executed. The break statement
is used to force control to leave the switch statement. The break
statement is not required, but if it's not present, control will fall
through to the next case. For instance, if the break was removed
from case four, then whenever k matched four both case four
and case five would be executed.

A special case called *default* can be used to mean "none of
the above." It need not be present. If it's not there and none of
the cases match, no action takes place within the switch. The
cases can be in any order, including the default case which need
not be last.

In general, the syntax of the switch statement is:

```
switch(integer_expr) {

        case constant_exp1:
                statement-1a;
                statement-1b;
                        .
                        .
                        .
                break; /*optional, but typical*/

        case constant_exp2:
                statement-2a;
                statement-2b;
                        .
                        .
                        .
                break;    /*ditto*/
            .
            .
            default:            /*optional case*/
```

```
    statement-xa;
    statement-xb;
           .
           .
           .
    break;
};
```

The expression in parentheses following the switch keyword must be evaluated to type integer. The case labels are constant expressions (like 5, or 60*60*24, etc.). Figure 5-7 is a flowchart of the switch statement's operation (with breaks). As an example, consider Listing 5-24. This program according to the following rules.

- If the input character is a carriage return, output carriage return and line feed.
- If the input character is form feed or vertical tab, output 20 new lines.
- Otherwise output the character.

In Listing 5-24 we used #define statements to give descriptive names to the values we were interested in. Had we not done this, the case labels would have been written as integer constants.

DO-WHILE LOOPS

The last loop statement we need to discuss is the do-while loop. The do-while loop is very similar to the while loop; the primary difference is that the loop control expression is at the end of the loop rather than the beginning. The syntax is:

```
do {
    statement-1;
    statement-2;
          .
          .
          .
    statement-k;
} while(expression);

next-sequential-statement;
```

124

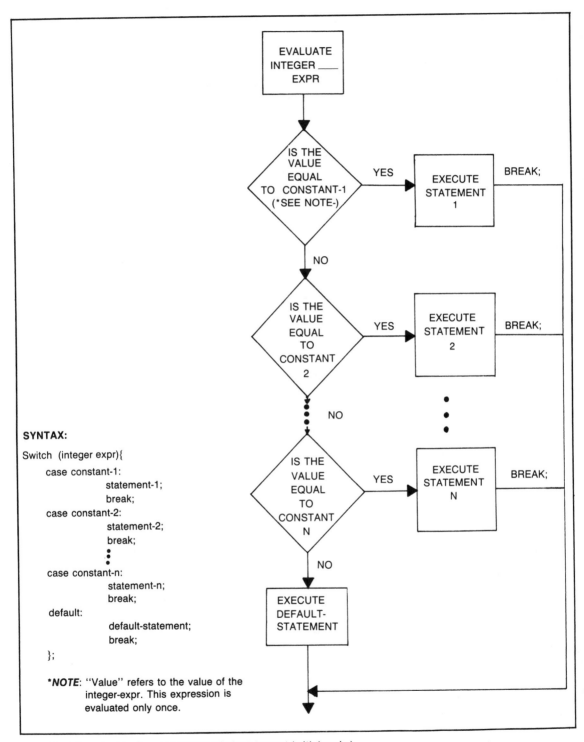

SYNTAX:

```
Switch  (integer expr){
      case constant-1:
                  statement-1;
                  break;
      case constant-2:
                  statement-2;
                  break;
              .
              .
      case constant-n:
                  statement-n;
                  break;
      default:
                  default-statement;
                  break;
      };
```

NOTE: ''Value'' refers to the value of the
integer-expr. This expression is
evaluated only once.

Fig. 5-7. A flowchart and syntax of the switch statement (with breaks).

Listing 5-24. An example of the switch statement.

```
#include <stdio.h>
#define FORMFEED   014  /* octal value of formfeed */
#define CR         015  /* octal value of carriage return */
#define VTAB       013  /* octal vertical tab */
#define LINEFEED   012  /* octal linefeed */

main()  {

        int c,i;
        while( (c = getchar() ) != EOF)
            switch(c)  {
                case CR:
                        putchar(CR);
                        putchar(LINEFEED);
                        break;

                case FORMFEED:
                case VTAB:
                        for(i = 0; i < 20; i++)
                                putchar('\n');
                        break;

                default:
                        putchar(c);
                        break;
            }
    }
```

Figure 5-8 shows the flow of the do-while statement.

The operation of the do-while is: (1) execute the statement (compound or simple) constituting the loop body; evaluate the expression; if the expression is nonzero, go back to step 1; and if expression is zero, exit the loop. Since the loop control expression is at the end of the loop, th eloop body is guaranteed to execute at least once.

The syntax shows the loop body as a compound statement; consequently, the loop body is enclosed in braces. If the loop body is a simple statement, braces are not required (but advisable). Thus:

```
do
     statement-1;
while (expression);
```

is perfectly acceptable syntax (to the compiler), but:

```
do {
     statement-1;
}while(expression);
```

is better (for humans).

126

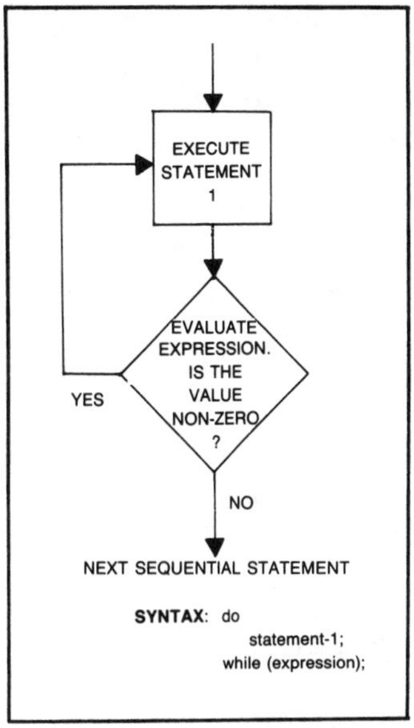

Fig. 5-8. A flowchart and syntax of the do-while statement.

EXECUTE STATEMENT 1

EVALUATE EXPRESSION. IS THE VALUE NON-ZERO ?

YES

NO

NEXT SEQUENTIAL STATEMENT

SYNTAX: do
    statement-1;
while (expression);

The unnecessary braces alert the reader that while (expression) is the end of a do-while loop, not the beginning of a while loop.

The do-while loop is a handy control construct when at least one execution of the loop body is required regardless of the value of the loop control expression.

LABELS AND GOTO STATEMENTS

If you've programmed in any dialect of BASIC or Fortran, you are familiar with the GOTO statement. In C goto is used in conjunction with a label.

A label can be inserted within a function by the syntax:

```
label_name:
```

A label name follows the same rules as variable names (Chapter 2): they begin with a letter (or underscore); and upper- and lowercase letters are considered different. When a label name is present, a statement of the form:

```
goto label_name:
```

can be executed. This causes control to immediately transfer to the labeled point of the program. This action is sometimes called a *jump*.

Goto is one word (i.e., not go to). The target of the goto—the labeled statement—must be in the same function as

127

the goto statement itself. Jumping from one function to another with a goto statement is not allowed.

To illustrate how labels and gotos look, consider the function "example" which illustrates the syntax (see Listing 5-25). "Start:" serves to label the function call n=search(s) and the goto statement causes control to jump there.

Gotos can be eliminated from programs. An extra test may be required to excise one from your program. At times, an extra variable may be added to the cost. The function example can be made "goto less" as shown in Listing 5-26. The price of eliminating the goto is the replication of the test n==ERROR.

The do-while loop was discussed in the last section. Here we needed to call the function search at least once, so the do-while makes sense.

If you are coming to C from a language bountiful in gotos (like BASIC or Fortran), make a conscious effort to write goto-less programs. It may be hard at first, but after a while it becomes easier.

A well-known example of when a goto is useful in C is when a deeply nested program must suddenly break from all of its loops. For instance:

```
while(...) {
    for(...) {
        switch(...) {




            .

            .

            .
```

Listing 5-25. Goto and label illustration.

```
#define ERROR  -1
#define OK      0

example(s) char s[];
{
        int n;

        start:                  /* a label */

                n = search(s);
                if(n == ERROR)  {
                        fix(s);
                        goto start;
                }
                return(OK);
}
```

Listing 5-26. Eliminating goto.

```
#define ERROR   -1
#define OK       0

example(s) char s[]; {

        int n;
        do  {
                n = search(s);
                if(n == ERROR);
                        fix(s);

        } while(n == ERROR);
        return  (OK);

}
```

```
        case 5:    /*break all loops */

                goto bigbreak;

        }

    }

}
bigbreak:
```

A goto is useful here since a break statement would only break the innermost switch.

Another useful case might be when complex error processing is done within a function. Perhaps the error processing code needs access to all the function's local variables to clean up things before the function exits. This code could be structured as follows:

```
function() {
        .
        .
        .
        if(something)
                goto error;
        .
        .
        .
        if(bad)
                goto error;
        .
        .
        .
        return;    /*the normal return*/
error:
        /*error processing*/
        .
        .
        .
}
```

SOME PREPROCESSOR ASIDES

When you write If statements in some languages they look like:

```
/*This is not C*/

if (expression) then
     statement-1;
else
     statement-2;
endif
```

C does not use the keywords *then* and *endif*. However, if you like these keywords C can be accomodating. Here's how to do it:

```
#define then
#define endif
```

These two #define statements instruct the preprocessor to substitute *nothing* for the words *then* and *endif*. In effect, these words are erased from the program before the actual compilation begins. Now If statements can be written as:

```
if (x>5) then
     y = 3*x;
else
     y = x;
endif
```

Also, C denotes compound statements by enclosing them in braces. Some languages require that such blocks of statements be bracketed by the keywords *begin* and *end*. Again, C can be accommodating:

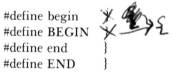

```
#define begin
#define BEGIN
#define end         }
#define END         }
```

Now compound statements can appear in the program as:

```
for (i=0; i < n; i++)
     begin
          x[i] = c;
          for (j = 0; j <m; j++)
                    begin
                       .
                       .
                       .


                    end

     end
```

130

We defined "begin" and "end" in such a way that it doesn't matter whether upper- or lowercase letters are used in the program. Note that "begin," "end," "then," and "endif" represent preprocessor *tokens*, not actual statements of the language. When they are used as in these examples, no semicolon follows them.

These examples illustrate the versatility accorded by the C preprocessor. However, if others are expected to read or maintain the program you write you should stick to standard C.

LOOP AND CONTROL EXAMPLES

There is nothing like an example to make everything crystal clear. In this section we've supplied several examples to illustrate the concepts of this chapter.

First let's examine the function *strcmp*, which compares two strings for equality (see Listing 5-27). This function just marches across the two strings, and as long as they are equal it merely checks to see if it has reached the end of string s. If it has, then clearly it has also reached the end of t (since s[i] == t[i]), hence it returns zero. If the test condition of the for loop ever fails the two strings are not equal. In this case value s[i]-t[i] is returned. This cannot be zero (why ?). By returning the difference of the two string elements, this function provides a signal as to which string comes first in the machine's collating sequence. Also, it illustrates that character variables can be used in arithmetic operations (subtraction, in this case) just like integers.

Strcpy is a function which copies strings. It is called as: strcpy(new, old), where the string old is copied into the string new. The order of new and old in the argument list is in agreement with what is generally used in the C community. This order is reminiscent of how assignment operations are performed.

Strcpy can be written with a for loop, as follows:

```
strcpy(new,old) char new[], old[]; {
    int i;
    for (i=0; new[i]=old[i]; i++ )
                        ;
}
```

Note that strcpy makes no attempt to check that the character array new[ ] is long enough to hold the string stored in old[ ]. This is the caller's responsibility and is something the caller can check before calling strcpy.

Compare the test expressions in strcpy and strcmp for loops. Strcpy is making an assignment; the for loop will terminate when the end-of-string marker is assigned. Strcmp is testing for equality; its for loop will terminate when the test is false.

The next example function, string_index, takes a string s and a character c as arguments and returns the index of the first occurrence of the character if it is in the string, and -1 if it is not (see Listing 5-28). The operation of this function depends on the fact that in C loop variables retain their value even after the loop execution is complete. Hence, the value of index returned by string-index x is the value that made the expression "s[index] != c" false. This value remains in the variable index even though execution of the for loop is complete.

The function *atoi* converts a character string to an integer. Its name is an acronym for "ASCII to integer." Let's assume we have a character string such as that shown in Fig. 5-9. As shown in the figure, the string represents $4 * 10^2 + 2 * 10 + 3$. The figure suggests the conversion strategy we'll use.

Atoi is shown in Listing 5-29. Some points to observe in atoi are:

Some points to observe in atoi are:

- The way spaces and tabs are skipped using a null statement within a for loop.
- In the switch statement note that: the value of i in s[i] is retained from the for loop. So we know that s[i] is neither a space nor a tab. There is no break between cases. The effect is that if s[i] == '-', both the sign = -1 and the i++ statements are executed. That is what is meant by "falling through" to the next case.
- In the while loop the expression s[i]-'0' converts the ASCII character in s[i] to its integer equivalent. This was discussed in Chapter 4. Once this conversion is made, the conversion strategy in Fig. 5-9 is used. If that strategy is not clear, try working through it with pencil and paper on an input string like "23."

Bubblesort is a sorting algorithm that can be used to sort an array of integers. Bubblesort works by making several passes over an array. On each pass, it performs the following logic: Sequentially compare adjacent cells of the array (e.g., cell-0 to cell-1, cell-1 to cell-2, etc.); if the cells are out of order, exchange their values. Suppose you are sorting numbers into increasing order. After one pass across the array the above procedure guarantees that the largest element is in the last cell of the array. Consequently, on the next pass you can ignore that element. After two passes the two largest elements are in their proper

Listing 5-27. Strcmp function.

```
strcmp(s,t) char s[], t[];  {

        /* Compare string s to string t.  Return 0 if the
           two strings are equal, nonzero otherwise */

        int i;

        for(i = 0; s[i] == t[i]; i++)
                if(s[i] == '\0')
                        return(0);

        return(s[i] - t[i]);

}
```

place and can be subsequently ignored. Hence, on each pass, we make fewer and fewer comparisons.

Figure 5-10 shows the effect of one pass of bubblesort on an array. The asterisks above the array cells indicate which elements are being compared in the current comparison. The sample array had five elements and pass 1 required four comparisons. Since the largest element is in place, pass 2 will require three comparisons, pass 3 requires two comparisons, and pass 4 (the last pass) will require only one. Listing 5-30 bubblesort in C.

EXERCISES

1. Write the overflow function:

```
overflow(line, line_size, num_chars_read)
        char line[];
```

Listing 5-28. The string_index function.

```
string_index(a,c)
        char s[], c;
{
        /* return the index of the first occurrence of c in
           string s, otherwise return -1 */

        int index;

        for(index = 0; s[index] != c; index++)
                if(s[index] == '\0')
                        return(-1);

        return(index);

}
```

133

Listing 5-29. The atoi-example.

```
atoi(s) char s[];  {
        /* Convert string s to integer.  S possibly has leading spaces
           or tabs, and may have a + or - sign */

        int i, sign, n;

        n = 0;
        i = 0;

        for(; s[i] == ' ' || s[i] == '\t'; i++)
                ;  /* skip spaces and tabs */

        sign = 1;
        switch(s[i])  {
                case '-': sign = -1;   /* The break statement is */
                case '+': i++;         /* intentionally omitted */

        }
        while(s[i] >= '0' && s[i] <= '9' )  {
                n = n * 10 + (s[i] - '0');
                i++;

        }
        return(sign*n);

}
```

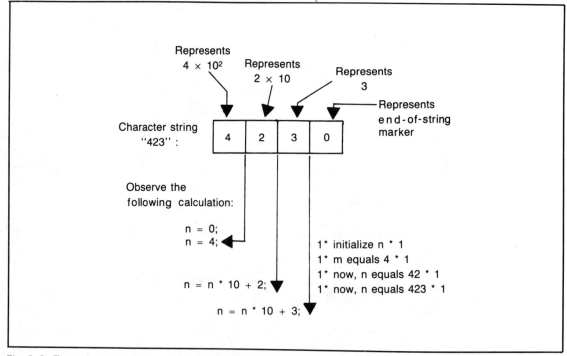

Fig. 5-9. The calculation approach for converting a digit string to an integer.

134

```
int line_size;
int num_chars_read;
```

Overflow will be passed

(a) line [ ], an array filled by getline.

(b) line size, the size of the array line.

(c) num_chars_read, the character count returned by getline.

Overflow returns TRUE if the input line was too long to fit into the array, FALSE otherwise.

2. Write the function:

```
reverse_string(instring,outstring)
        char instring[];
        char outstring[];
```

which makes a reversed copy of instring in outstring. For example, if instring is "the," outstring is "eht." Assume outstring is long enough to hold all the characters.

3. Write the function:

```
reverse(string)
        char string[];
```

which reverses the string in place. (Hint: use strlen to determine how long the string is.)

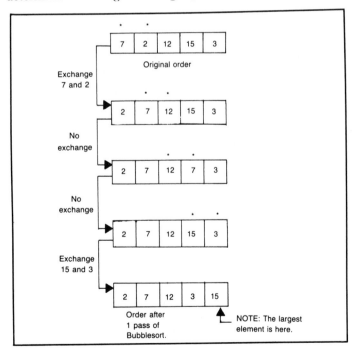

Fig. 5-10. One pass of bubblesort on an array.

Listing 5-30. The bubblesort function.

```
bubblesort (x,n)
        int x[];          /* the array to be sorted */
        int n;            /* the number of array elements */

        /* sort array into increasing order */

    {

        int i,j,temp;
        int lastindex;

        /* lastindex will be initialized to n-1.  Remember
           C arrays are indexed from 0 to n-1 */

        for(i = 0, lastindex = n-1; lastindex > 0; --lastindex)
            for(j = 0; j < lastindex; j++)
                if(x[j] > x[j+1])  {
                            /* exhchange x[j] and x[j+1] */
                            temp = x[j];        /* save x[j] */
                            x[j] = x[j+1];
                            x[j+1] = temp;
                        }
    }
```

4. Write a function called read_line which behaves like getline except that it leaves the new line character out of the input array.

5. If getline is not available as a library function on your system, test (and modify if necessary) the version presented in the chapter. Save a correct version of the function in a file called getline.c. That file will be used later in the text.

6. Write a program to test getword. You may need to modify the #define EOL statement for the function to work properly on your system. (Refer to the discussion at the end of the getline section). Save an operable version of the function's source code in a file called "getword.c." That file will be used later in the text.

7. If your system supports I/O redirection:
   (a) Write a program which reads lines from the standard input, displaying them on the standard output. The program should pause when one screen of data is displayed and continue when the user strikes any key. By redirecting I/O, use the program to display a file.

   (b) Modify the program written above to keep track of the number of lines read and characters read. Display the line count and character count at each program pause.

Chapter 6

Pointers and Arrays

Arrays were introduced in Chapter 2. We'll now discuss arrays in more detail and introduce multidimensional arrays.

It is quite natural in C to discuss arrays and pointers simultaneously. Any expression that involves an array can be written as an expression that uses pointers instead. Pointers are widely used in C. Pointers allow functions to actually change the value of variables in other functions, and they allow for the efficient processing of arrays. Let's begin by covering the basic concepts of pointers.

BASICS OF POINTERS

All objects in a program (that is, the integers, floats, characters, and so on), physically reside at some location in the computer's memory. Consider the following declarations:

```
int i = 7;
int j = 10;
int k = 15;
```

Assume that these variables have their values stored in memory locations as shown in Fig. 6-1; the value of i (7) is stored at location 62, the value of j (10) is stored at location 64, and the value of k (15) is stored at memory location 66.

Memory contents	Memory address	Object stored at this location
7	62	int i
10	64	tnt j
15	66	int k

Fig. 6-1. Memory image resulting from the declarations: int i=7; int j=10; and int k=15.

In your program you can determine the memory location of an object (the address of the object) by using the C *address-of* operator. This operator is denoted by an ampersand (&). Hence, the statements:

```
point_i = &i;
point_j = &j;
point_k = &k;
```

assign the addresses of i, j, and k to the variables point_i, point_j, and point_k, respectively. Under our assumptions point_i now contains the value 62, point_j the value 64, and point_k the value 66. Variables used to hold the addresses of objects are called *pointers*. We say that these variables point to memory locations.

If you have a valid pointer to an object you can access the value of the object indirectly by using the pointer. Conceptually you are supplying a memory address and instructing the computer to fetch the value stored at that address. This is done by using the C *indirection* operator which is denoted by the asterisk(*). Hence, the expression:

```
*point_i
```

means: "point_i is the address of an object; fetch the value stored at that address." Thus, the value of *point_i in this example is seven, because point_i is pointing to i, and i has the value of seven.

For these statements to work correctly, the pointer variables must be properly declared. To declare the pointer variables used here, the following declaration is required:

```
              int *point_i, *point_j, *point_k;
```

The asterisk preceding each variable name indicates that the variable is being used to point to an int. It is a logical way to write the declaration, in the sense that if point_i is a pointer to an int, then *point_i is an int. The expression *point_i can appear anywhere that an integer can legally appear.

Pointers to other types of objects are declared in a similar manner. For instance:

```
char *s, *t;      /* Declares s and t as pointers to char*/
float *fp;        /* Declares fp to be a pointer to a float*/
```

With these declarations s references the address of a character, and *s references an actual character.

Consider how pointers are used in programs by examining Listing 6-1. Try running this program on your system to observe its output. Note that when two pointers are declared as pointing to the same type of objects (as point1 and point2 both point to int), it is possible to assign the pointer values. This is exemplified by the statement:

```
              point1 = point2;
```

Listing 6-1. Pointer Usage.

```
main()  {  /* pointer examples */

     int i = 10;  /* Declare and initialize two ints */
     int j = 15;

     int *point1, *point2;  /* Declare int pointers */

     int k, m;

     point1 = &i;  /* point1 now points to i */
     k = *point1;  /* The value 10 is assigned to k */

     point2 = &j;  /* point2 is pointing to j */
     m = *point2;  /* the value 15 is assigned to m */

     printf("k = %d  *point1 = %d  \n", k, *point1);
     printf("m = %d  *point2 = %d  \n", m, *point2);

     point1 = point2;  /* Now point1 is pointing to j--the
                           same thing that point2 is pointing to. */

     printf("*point1 = %d  *point2 = %d  \n", *point1,  *point2);


}
```

This statement causes the pointer on the left side of the assignment operator to point to the same thing as the one on the right side.

Pointer variables can also be given various storage classes. For example:

```
dummy() {

    register char *s;
    extern int *p;
        .
        .
        .

}
```

The first declaration states that s will hold the address of a character and that a machine register should be allocated for s. The second states that p will hold the address of an integer and that p is defined external to the function dummy (see Chapter 3).

When we discussed the register storage class in Chapter 3 we stated that some objects will not fit in a register. For instance, a declaration:

```
register double y;   /*WRONG*/
```

is illegal because doubles are too big for machine registers. However, it is perfectly legal to declare:

```
register double *yp;
```

Here a register is requested for the address of a double, not for the double itself.

The address-of operator (&), and the C indirection operator (*) are both unary operators (they have one operand). Further, the & operator can only be applied to variables and array elements. You cannot take the address of a constant:

```
pointf =  &7.2 ;  /* illegal */
```

nor can you take the address of an expression:

```
int x;

p = &( x+ 5);  /* illegal */
```

nor can you take the address of a register:

Listing 6-2. A version of the function bigger.

```
bigger(x,y,status)
        int x,y,status;  {

if(x > y)
        status = TRUE;

else
        status = FALSE;

}
```

```
wrong() {
    register int index;
    int *p;

    p = &index;  /* illegal, can't take the
                        address of a register */
}
```

Finally, C guarantees that the value zero is never a valid memory address for a pointer variable. This fact is often used by functions that return pointers. When a pointer value of zero is returned, it signals that some error has occurred.

PASSING POINTERS TO FUNCTIONS

In Chapter 3 we discussed the call by value method of passing arguments to functions. Now reconsider that notion within the context of pointers.

Listing 6-3. Main calling bigger.

```
#define TRUE    1
#define FALSE   0
#include <stdio.h>

main() {
        int x, y, status;

        x = 10;         /* set x to be bigger */
        y = 1;      /*    than y */

        status = FALSE;

        bigger(x,y,status);

        if(status == TRUE)
                printf("x is bigger than y\n");
        else
                printf("x is not bigger than y\n");

}
```

Consider a function called bigger, which is passed three arguments. Bigger compares the first two arguments and sets the third argument to TRUE if the first argument is larger than the second. Examine the version in Listing 6-2. Then consider a function main that calls bigger in Listing 6-3. Stop for a moment and examine the function main. What gets printed by this main function?

If you said "x is bigger than y" gets printed, you need to review call by value. A quick review follows.

Just before the function bigger is called in main, the values of x, y, and status have been initialized. They are stored somewhere in memory, shown in Fig. 6-2A. As bigger is entered it gets its own private copies of the arguments (i.e., call by value). These private copies are stored at different locations in memory than the values used by main, shown in Fig. 6-2B.

As a result of bigger's execution, its private copy of the variable status is set to TRUE (Fig. 6-2C). But this has no effect upon the copy of status used by main. Hence, main's copy of status is still FALSE, so it prints "x is not bigger than y."

Now, try it again using pointers (Listing 6-4). Figure 6-3(A) shows main's variables for this case. It looks just like Figure 6-2(A). When main calls bigger—bigger(x,y,&status)— the argument &status causes the address of main's status variable to be passed to the function bigger. Upon entering bigger the values of its private copies of the variables are shown in Fig. 6-3B. When the line:

```
*status = TRUE;
```

is executed in bigger, the pointer stored in bigger's copy of status is used to actually change the value of main's variable status. This is shown in Fig. 6-3C. This time main prints "x is bigger than y."

You can see that if a called function must actually change a variable's value in the calling function, a pointer must be passed. In this way pointers serve as another communications path between functions.

If a function is written to accept a pointer as its argument, say:

```
something(pn) int *pn; {

    /* do something with the pointer pn */

}
```

142

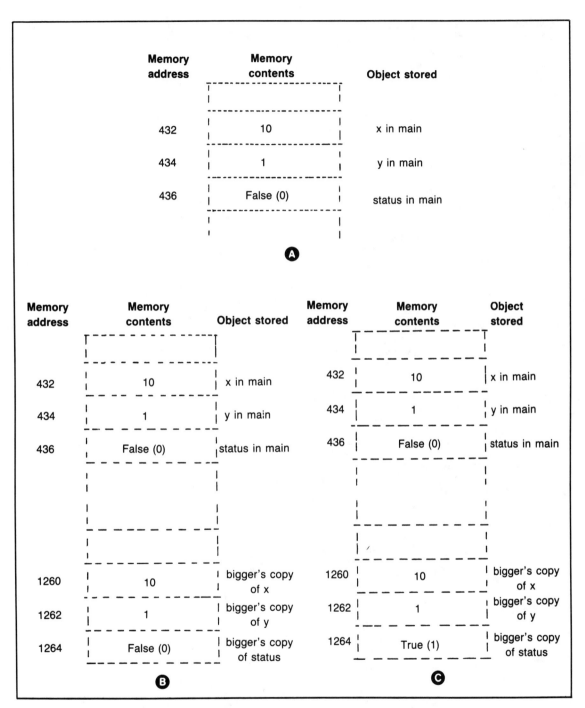

Fig. 6-2(A). Main's variables just before function bigger is called. (B) value of variables on entry of bigger. (C) value of variables after "status=TRUE," is executed in bigger.

Listing 6-4. Pointer version of bigger.

```
          #define TRUE    1
          #define FALSE   0
          #include <stdio.h>

          main()  {

                  int x,y;
                  int status;

                  x = 10;
                  y = 1;
                  status = FALSE;

                  bigger(x,y,&status);   /* Note the address-of operator
                                             with status */

                  if(status == TRUE)
                          printf("x is bigger than y\n");

                  else
                          printf("x is not bigger than y\n");
          }

  bigger(x,y,status)
          int x,y;
          int *status;   /* Note the pointer declaration */
  {

          if(x > y)
                  *status = TRUE;
          else
                  *status = FALSE;
  }
```

there are a few ways a function calling "something" can arrange
to pass the pointer. One way is the following:

```
      main()  {

          int k;

          something( &k ); /* pass the address of the int k */
      }
```

A second way is:

```
        main()  {

            int k;
            int *j;

            /* make the pointer j point to an int */
            j = &k;
            something(j);  /* pass the pointer j */

        }
```

144

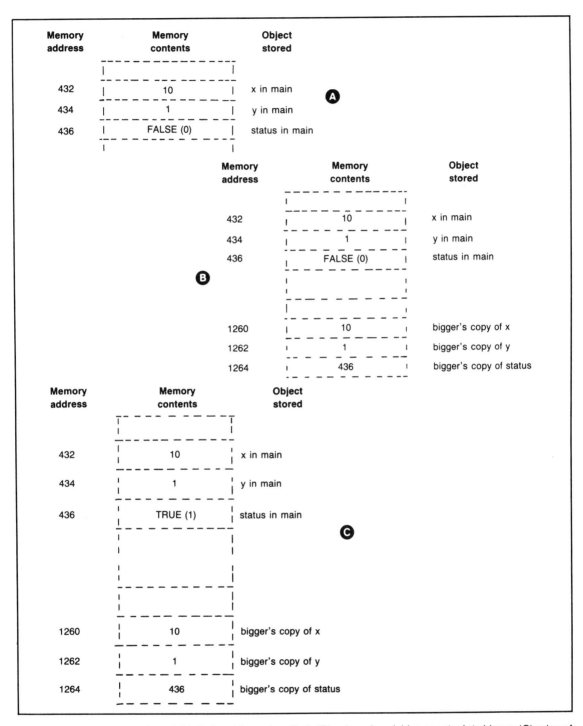

Memory address	Memory contents	Object stored
432	10	x in main
434	1	y in main
436	FALSE (0)	status in main

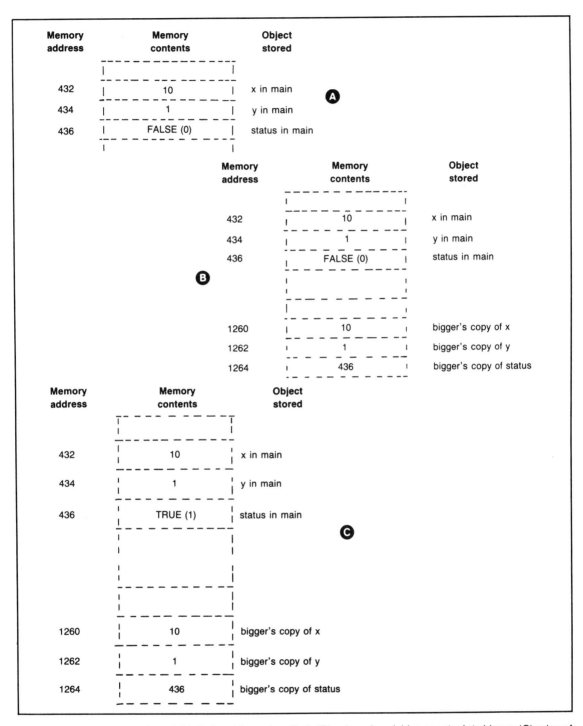 **A**

Memory address	Memory contents	Object stored
432	10	x in main
434	1	y in main
436	FALSE (0)	status in main
1260	10	bigger's copy of x
1262	1	bigger's copy of y
1264	436	bigger's copy of status

B

Memory address	Memory contents	Object stored
432	10	x in main
434	1	y in main
436	TRUE (1)	status in main
1260	10	bigger's copy of x
1262	1	bigger's copy of y
1264	436	bigger's copy of status

C

Fig. 6-3(A). Value of main's variable before bigger is called. (B) value of variables on entry into bigger. (C) value of variables after ✴"status =TRUE"; is executed in bigger.

145

A third way is:

```
main() {

    int values[10];

    something(values); /* An array name is automatically
                          a pointer.  We'll discuss this
                          in the next section */
}
```

It is incorrect to pass a pointer to a function like this:

```
main() {

    int *j;

    something(j); /* Incorrect pointer passing */
}
```

In the last case j is certainly a pointer, but it has never been initialized to point to anything! Because it is an automatic variable in the function main, its value is garbage until it is initialized. Thus it may be pointing anywhere! Passing an uninitialized pointer to a function can cause hard-to-find program errors.

Pointers are routinely passed to functions when a function must return more than one value. Within a function, we know the return statement allows one value to be returned to a calling function; when a function must return more than one value to its caller, the use of the return statement alone is insufficient. One way in which more than one value can be passed back to a calling function is to use pointers. With this method the calling function will pass pointers indicating where values calculated by the called function should be stored. The called function can then store the values indirectly through the pointers. The minmax function in Listing 6–5 illustrates this use. It finds both the minimum and maximum of an array and passes these values back by using pointers supplied by the calling function.

Program Listing 6–6 tests the minmax function. It prompts for integer data, reads the data into an array, then calls minmax to find the minimum and maximum integers in the array. To compile the program, you need to have the files minmax.c, getline.c, and atoi.c on your disk. Minmax.c should contain the minmax function shown above. Getline.c and atoi.c contain the functions written in Chapter 5.

Another instance in which pointers are routinely passed to functions is when an array name is the argument in a function call. Arrays are not actually passed to functions. That is,

146

Listing 6-5. The function Minmax.

```
minmax(x,xsize,min,max)

        int x[];        /* the array to be searched */
        int xsize;      /* the number of elements in x[] */
        int *min;       /* a pointer to where the min goes */
        int *max;       /* a pointer to where the max goes */

(   /* find min and max of array x */
        int i, lmin, lmax;

        lmin = lmax = x[0];

        for(i = 1; i < xsize; i++)  (
                if( x[i] > lmax )
                        lmax = x[i];
                if( x[i] < lmin )
                        lmin = x[i];
        }

        *min = lmin;
        *max = lmax;

}
```

Listing 6-6. Testing minmax.

```
#include <stdio.h>

/* This program uses getline and atoi as written in Chapter 5.
   If these functions are provided on your system, then
   remove the next two #include statements
*/

#include "getline.c"
#include "atoi.c"

#include "minmax.c"

main() (
int min_value, max_value;
int value[10];
int i;
char data[10];

for(i=0; i<10; i++ ) (
        printf("\nEnter an integer>");
        getline(data,10);
        value[i] = atoi(data);
}

minmax(value, 10, &min_value, &max_value);

printf("\nThe integers entered are:\n");
for(i=0; i<10; i++ )
        printf("%d   ", value[i]);
printf("\n\nThe min value is %d, the max value is %d\n",min_value,max_value);


}
```

functions do not receive private copies of all of the array elements; rather, the C compiler arranges for a pointer to the beginning of the array to be passed. For instance, in the call: getline(data, 10) you know that "data" is the name of an array. Further, the function getline actually changed the value of the array elements, that is, it filled the array with input characters.) This was possible because a pointer to the array was actually passed to getline. This is an example of the bond between arrays and pointers. In the next section, this bond will be discussed in more detail.

ARRAYS AND ADDRESS ARITHMETIC

Consider a character array called string defined as:

char string [ ] = "This is a string";

These characters are stored contiguously in memory; Fig. 6-4 depicts this. In the figure arbitrary memory addresses (51, 52, ... 67) are used. Now, suppose that p is a pointer to a character, declared by:

```
char *p;
```

If you set p to point to the zeroth element in the array with the statement:

```
p  = &string[0];
```

then according to Fig. 6-4, p will hold the address 51. You can now access the character stored at location 51 by using the notation:

```
*p
```

If one is added to p, p will equal 52, the address of the next character in the array. Again, the notation *p allows you to access this character.

By performing arithmetic on the pointer in this way, you can march the pointer across the character array accessing individual elements with the indirection operator. For example, Listing 6-7 prints the string.

In this example the address-of operator was used as:

```
p = &string[0];
```

This points p to the beginning of the array. The indirection operator was used to end the test for the end-of-string and to

Memory address	Memory contents	Object's name	
51	T	string[0]	
52	h	string[1]	
53	i	string[2]	
54	s	string[3]	
55		string[4]	1 a blank space *1
56	i	string[5]	
57	s	string[5]	
58		string[7]	
59	a	string[8]	
60		string[9]	
61	s	string[10]	
62	t	string[11]	
63	r	string[12]	
64	i	string[13]	
65	n	string[14]	
66	g	string[15]	
67	/0	string[16]	1* end-of-string marker *1

Fig. 6-4. Storage resulting from the declaration: char string [] = "This is a string";.

output the character with putchar. The increment operator (++p) performs the pointer arithmetic and positions p to point to the next array element.

The link between pointers and arrays in C is really much tighter than this example shows. For instance, whenever an array is declared, the name of the array (without brackets) is automatically initialized to point to the zeroth array element. So, the previous program could be written as Listing 6-8. This notion is true for all types of arrays. For instance, if:

```
int num[5];
```

is declared, num is initialized to point to num[0]. Figure 6-5 indicates this relationship.

Listing 6-7. Printing a string using pointers.

```
#include <stdio.h>

char string[] = "This is a string";

main()  {
        char *p;
        p = &string[0];         /* set p to point to the beginning of string */

        while(*p != '\0')  {    /* loop until end-of-string */
                putchar(*p);      /* print the char p currently points to */
                ++p;              /* make p point to the next char */

        }

}
```

Though array names such as "num" and "string" are initialized as pointers to the beginning of the arrays, it should be noted that these names are not variables. They are like symbolic constants. You cannot assign other values to them. So statements like:

```
num = 15;          /* WRONG */
string = x + y;    /* WRONG */
```

are illegal. However, they can be used on the right side of an assignment statement. For instance, with the declarations:

```
int num[5], *p, *r;
char string[17], *p;
```

Listing 6-8. Alternate string printing example.

```
#include <stdio.h>
char string[] = "This is a string";

main()  {
        char  *p;

        p = string; /*"string" automatically holds the address of string[0] */

        while( *p != '\0' )  {
                putchar(*p);
                p++;

        }

}
```

150

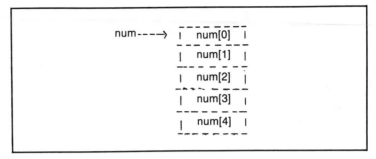

Fig. 6-5. Storage allocation resulting from the declaration: int num[5];.

the statements:

```
r = num;
p = num + 1;
s = string + 7;
```

cause r to point to num[0], p to point to num[1], and s to point to string[7];

Let's backtrack a little and examine some of the arbitrary memory addresses used in previous examples. In Fig. 6-1 we show an example of three integers being stored contiguously in memory. The arbitrary addresses we used were 62, 64, and 66. In Fig. 6-4 we show an example of 17 characters being stored contiguously in memory. The arbitrary addresses there were 51, 52, ..., 67. The fact that contiguous addresses for the integers differ by two, while the contiguous addresses for characters differ by one, is not unusual. It is quite conceivable that the machine in question addresses memory by bytes and that an integer takes two bytes to store while a character takes only one byte. In this case the addresses of contiguous integers would increase by two while contiguous character addresses would increase by one. In fact, if the array x is defined as:

```
double x[5];
```

the memory layout of these five contiguous variables may differ by four or even eight. This all depends on the machine and the compiler you are using.

Fortunately, when address arithmetic is performed in C all these size differences are taken into account by the compiler. As the programmer you don't have to worry about them. This means that if p points to an array element (of any type), then p+1 points to the next array element, and p−1 points to the previous array element. In general, p+i points i elements after p, and p−i points i elements before p. We illustrate what this means with a few C statements. With the declarations:

```
double x[5];
double *xp, *yp;
```

the statement:

```
xp = x;
```

copies the address of x[0] into the pointer variable xp. Now the statement:

```
yp = xp+1;
```

makes yp point to x[1] (xp still points to x[0]). Even if a particular machine uses eight bytes to store a double, the pointer is incremented by the correct amount.

The relationship between arrays and pointers is becoming apparent. Observe as we discuss it further.

If num is an array defined as:

```
int num[5];
```

then Table 6-1 specifies the relationship between array/index notation and pointer notation. In each row of the table column 1 and column 3 represent different notations to access the same array element. The relationship is strengthened by the fact that these notations can be used interchangeably. That is, you can declare an array, then address the elements using pointer notation; or, you can declare a pointer then address the elements it points to using array/index notation. Examine the following example for clarification. Program Listing 6-9 searches a string looking for the last occurrence of a specified character.

Note that even though the argument s is declared to be an array of type char, it is quite acceptable to reference the array elements using pointer notation. We have done this in the first for loop. Since s is a pointer to the beginning of the array, s+j is a pointer to s[j], and *(s+j) is the value of the element s[j]. When this value is \0 (the end-of-string marker), the for loop

**Table 6-1 Relationship Between Array/Index
Notation and Pointer Notation Using Declaration: int num[5];**

Array/Index Notation	Address of The Array Element	Pointer Notation To Access The Array Element
num[0]	num	*num
num[1]	num+1	*(num+1)
num[2]	num+2	*(num+2)
num[3]	num+3	*(num+3)
num[4]	num+4	*(num+4)

Listing 6-9. String searching, version one.

```
lastchar(s,c)
      char s[];
      char c;  {

      /* Find the last occurrence of the character stored in c
         in the string s.  Return its index or -1 if c is not in s */

      int j;

      /* Position j at the end of the string */
      for(j =0; *(s+j) != '\0';  j++)
                    ;

      /* Now backup across s[] looking for c */
      for (--j;  j >= 0  && s[j]  != c;  --j)
                        ;

      return (j);

}
```

terminates. In the second for loop we chose to reference the array element as s[j]. Again, everything is consistent and well defined.

Finally, the return statement returns the value of j. If c was present the condition s[j]!=c came up false. Hence s[j]==c must be true and j is the right index. If c was not in the string, j is the first value that made j>=0 false, so j must be −1. A version of lastchar that uses pointer notation exclusively is in Listing 6-10.

In this version the first for loop begins by initializing the local variable sp to point to the string to be searched (sp=s).

Listing 6-10. String searching, version two.

```
lastchar(s,c)

        char *s;
        char c;  {

        char *sp;

        /* Position the pointer sp at the end of the string */
        for(sp=s;  *sp != '\0'; sp++)
                        ;

        /* Now backup across string looking for c */
        for( --sp; sp >= s  && *sp != c ; --sp  )
                          ;
        return (sp - s );

        }
```

Then a check is made to see if the end of the string has been reached ($*sp != '\o'$). If we're not at the end yet, the null body of the for loop is executed, then the pointer is incremented to point to the next character in the string (sp++).

The next for loop marches the pointer backwards across the string so long as:

```
sp>=s && *sp != c
```

is true. The first of these conditions (sp>=s) ensures that the pointer has not backed past the beginning of the string. The second ($*sp != c$) checks to see if the character has been found yet. (Why must the tests occur in that order?) When this for loop terminates, the value sp−s is returned. This value will be the desired result—either the index of the last occurrence of c in the string, or −1 if no match occurred. To verify this in your own mind, consider the case implied by the call lastchar("the", 't'). The last occurrence of 't' in "the" occurs at index 0. When the for loop terminates in this case, sp will equal s, so sp−s is zero. Figure 6-6 tracks the position of the pointers for the call lastchar("example", 'a').

You have examined two versions of a function called lastchar. In the first version, the format parameter s was declared

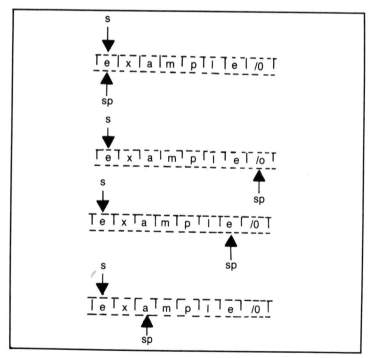

Fig. 6-6. Pointer snapshots for the function call: lastchar("example", 'a').

as char s[ ]. In the second version, s was declared as char *s. The declarations:

```
char s[];
```

and

```
char *s;
```

can be used interchangeably when they declare formal parameters to functions. Whenever an array name is passed to a function, what is actually passed is a pointer to the beginning of the array. So within the function's definition the formal parameter representing the array can be declared as either an array or as a pointer. A pointer is passed regardless.

Further, a portion of an array can be passed to a function. To do this you need only pass a pointer to the element of the array you wish the function to begin with. Program Listing 6-11 exemplifies this. On the first iteration of the for loop strlen is passed a pointer to digits[0], the beginning of the array. On successive iterations strlen is passed pointers to digits[1], then digits[2], and so on. On these iterations strlen computes the length of the respective portion of the array. The program prints:

Listing 6-11. Passing portions of an array to a function.

```
strlen(s) char s[];   {

        int i;

        for( i = 0; s[i]  != '\0';  i++)
                        ;
        return(i);
}

char digits[] = "0123456789";

main()   {

        int i, count;

        for(i = 0;  i < 10;  i++)   {

                count = strlen( &digits[i] );
                printf("There are %d digits in %s\n", count, &digits[i]);

        }

}
```

```
There are 10 digits in 0123456789
There are 9 digits in 123456789
There are 8 digits in 23456789
There are 7 digits in 3456789
```

POINTER EXPRESSIONS AND PRECEDENCE

You have seen that pointer arithmetic is completely consistent. That is, if p points to an array of objects, then regardless of the size of the object, p+1 points to the next object, p—i points i objects before p, etc.

You have seen some pointer expressions already. Namely, with the declarations:

```
char s[100];
char *sp;
char c;
```

you know that:

```
sp = s;   /* equivalently sp= &s[0]; */
```

causes sp to point to s[0]:

```
sp++;   /* equivalently sp = sp + 1; or sp += 1; */
```

causes sp to point to the next element of s, and:

```
c = *sp;
```

causes the character being pointed to by sp to be assigned to c. These are basic pointer expressions. The remainder of this section expands your repertoire of pointer expressions.

The expression:

```
*sp++
```

involves two operators (*, ++). Its value is the character being pointed to by sp. Because the increment operator is written in postfix notation, the pointer sp is incremented after the value is taken.

When you use the arithmetic operators to perform pointer arithmetic in conjunction with the pointer operators (*,&), you must be aware of the relative precedence of the operators. The precedence of the pointer operators is higher than the arithmetic or assignment operators, and at the same level as the increment and decrement operators. Table 6-2 illustrates exactly where

156

Table 6-2 Precedence of the Arithmetic, Relational, And Pointer Operators.

Operator Use	Operator Symbol	Associativity
function calls array references	() []	Left To Right
address-of indirection unary minus increment, decrement cast, sizeof negation	& * − ++ −− (type) sizeof !	Right To Left
multiply, divide modulus	* / %	Left To Right
add, subtract	+ −	Left To Right
relational	< <= > >=	Left To Right
equality, inequality	== !=	Left To Right
logical connective and	&&	Left To Right
logical connective or	||	Left To Right
conditional	?:	Right To Left
assignment	= += −= *= /= %=	Right To Left
sequential execution	,	Left To Right

Note: Operators between horizontal bars have same precedence and associativity. Top of table is the highest precedence operators.

these operators fall within the precedence hierarchy relative to all the operators you have seen so far.

As an example, you can write the string copy function (strcpy) using pointer notation as:

```
strcpy(to,from)
    char *to,*from; {
    char *t,*f;

    /* initialize the local pointer variables */

    t = to;
    f = from;

    /* copy the string */

    while (*t++ = *f++)
        ;
}
```

Note that the loop control expression of the while loop performs all the work. The expression: *t++ = *f++ uses the assignment operator to copy the character pointed to by f into the character pointed to by t. Both pointers are then incremented to point to the next cell of their respective character arrays. The value of the expression: *t++ = *f++ is the value of the character copied. When the end-of-string marker is copied the expression has the value zero and the while loop completes.

Two character pointers are passed to strcpy. Because these pointers are passed by value, strcpy gets a private copy of the pointers. Hence, strcpy is free to alter its private copies of the pointers without affecting the value of the pointers in the calling function. So, strcpy could be written as in Listing 6-12. In this case, even though strcpy increments both the passed pointers it is only incrementing its private copies. The pointers maintained by the calling function are not affected.

You can see that the pointer expression *sp++ is useful in C. Similar expressions are:

```
*sp--
*++sp
*--sp
```

The first (*sp−−) gets the value of the object pointed to by sp, then decrements the pointer to point to the previous object of the same type. The second (*++sp) increments the pointer, then fetches the value of the object being pointed to. The third (*−−sp) decrements the pointer, then fetches the value being pointed to.

Parentheses can be used to change the order in which the operations occur. Whereas:

```
*sp++
```

causes the pointer to be incremented,

```
(*sp)++
```

causes the value pointed to by sp to be incremented. In this case the value of the pointer is not changed.

With the declarations:

Listing 6-12. Another version of strcpy.

```
strcpy(to, from)   char *to, *from;   {
        while(*to++ = *from++)
                        ;

    }
```

158

```
int j, i = 10;
int *ip;
```

the statements:

```
ip = &i;
j = (*ip)++;
```

assign j the value 10 and leave i with the value 11. The pointer ip is left pointing to the variable i. With the same set of declarations, the statements:

```
ip = &i;
j = ++(*ip);
```

assign j the value 11, and leave i with the value 11. Again, the value of the pointer is not changed.

The expressions:

```
(*sp)++
*sp = *sp + 1
*sp += 1
```

are all equivalent. They increment the object being pointed to and leave the pointer unchanged. Analogously, the expressions:

```
++(*sp)
--(*sp)
(*sp)--
```

increment or decrement values being pointed to. They too leave the pointer unchanged. Table 6-3 summarizes these C idioms.

Other useful pointer expressions are those that involve relational operators. For instance, the declarations:

```
#define BUFSIZE 512
char buf[BUFSIZE];
char *bufp = buf;
```

define an array called buf with 512 elements. Additionally, a pointer called bufp is defined and initialized to point to buf[0]. Because the last legitimate element of the array is buf[BUFSIZE −1], the last legitimate pointer value to this array is buf+BUFSIZE−1.

When developing C code to access an array with pointer notation, the relational operators are used to ensure that you are pointing at the array. For example, to determine how many e's are stored in the array buf, you can write:

Table 6-3. Pointer Expressions Using
* ++ −−Assume Declarations char c, *sp;

Expression	Is Pointer Changed?	Effect
c = *sp++	yes	Assign the value pointed to by sp to c, then increment the pointer.
c = *++sp	yes	Increment the pointer, then assign c the value being pointed to.
c = *sp−−	yes	Assign the value pointed to by sp to c, then increment the pointer.
c = *−−sp	yes	Decrement the pointer, then assign c the value being pointed to.
c = (*sp)++	no	Fetch the value pointed to by sp and assign the value to c. Now, increment the value being pointed to.
c = ++(*sp)	no	Increment the value being pointed to by sp. Assign the new value to c.
c = (*sp)−−	no	Fetch the value being pointed to by sp and assign the value to c. Now decrement the value being pointed to.
c = −−(*sp)	no	Decrement the value pointed to by sp. Assign the new value to c.

```
for(bufp=buf; bufp<buf+BUFSIZE ;bufp++)
    if(*bufp == 'e')
            ecount++;
```

The test "bufp < buf+BUFSIZE" remains true as long as bufp is less than or equal to buf+BUFSIZE−1. In other words, the test is true as long as a legitimate array element is being pointed to.

If p and q are two pointers that point to the same array the expression p−q is meaningful. It tells how many array elements are between the two pointers. Consider Fig. 6-7, where a character array is shown. In the figure we indicate that q points to a, and p points to d. With standard address arithmetic, note that p==q+3. In this case, p−q equals three.

A STACK EXAMPLE

In this section we will implement a data structure called a *stack*. We'll do this by writing several functions that maintain the stack and provide status information about it.

A stack is a data structure that works like the plate stacking device in a cafeteria. When a new plate is placed upon the cafeteria stack, all the other plates are pushed down to

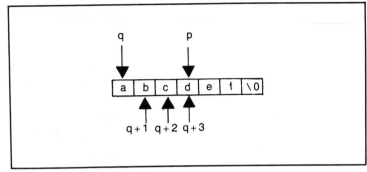

Fig. 6-7. The relationship of two pointers: char *p, *q; pointing to different elements of the same array.

accommodate the new one. When a plate is removed from the stack the other plates pop up toward the top of the stack. A stack satisfies the property that the last object pushed onto the stack is the first object removed from the stack. This property is called *last in first out,* (LIFO). Data stacks are often used in programs to provide temporary storage.

For the data stack, we'll write the following functions:

- push(data):   push the data onto the top of the stack
- pop( ):   pop the data off of the stack
- stacksize( ):   report the number of items on the stack
- stackempty( ):   return TRUE if the stack is empty, FALSE otherwise
- stackfull( ):   return TRUE if the stack is full, FALSE otherwise
- clearstack( ):   clear the stack of all items
- printstack( ):   print the contents of the stack

We'll define the stack to hold integers, and give it a maximum size of STACKSIZE (Listing 6-13).

Most of the pointer expressions discussed in the last section are used in stack functions. Push uses the expression $*sp++ = n$ to store an integer onto the stack and to increment the stack pointer to point to the next free slot. Pop uses $*--sp$ to return the value of the top stack element. Because sp points to a free slot, the prefix use of $--$ backs sp up to point to an already filled slot. The indirection operator then fetches that element.

Both stackfull( ) and stackempty( ) use relational expressions involving the stack pointer. To determine if the stack is full, the expression:

```
sp >= stack + STACKSIZE
```

161

Listing 6-13. Stack functions.

```
#define TRUE 1
#define FALSE 0

#define STACKSIZE       80
int stack[STACKSIZE];   /* STORAGE FOR THE STACK */

int *sp = stack;

push(n) int n; {
        if(stackfull() ) {
                printf("push: Error - Stack full\n");
                return(0);
        }
        else{
                *sp++ = n;
                return(n);
        }
}

pop(){
        if(stackempty()) {
                printf("pop: Error - Stack empty\n");
                return(0);
        }
        else
                return( *--sp);
}

clearstack(){
        sp = stack;
}

stackempty(){
        return( sp==stack ? TRUE: FALSE );
}

stackfull() {
        return( sp >= stack + STACKSIZE ? TRUE : FALSE);
}

stacksize() {
        return( sp-stack );
}

printstack() {
        int i;

        putchar('\n');
        i = stacksize();
        while( i-- > 0 )
                printf("%d\n", *( stack + i) );
}
```

is used. Because the last legitimate element of the stack is stack[STACKSIZE-1], the last legitimate pointer value is stack+STACKSIZE-1. Similarly, stackempty uses sp==stack to determine if the pointer indicates that stack[0] is still free.

The function stacksize uses the subtraction operator with pointer operands (i.e., sp-stack) to report the number of elements present on the stack. Finally, printstack prints the elements on the stack one integer per line. Note the postfix decrement operator in the while loop of printstack:

```
while( i-- >0)
        printf("%d\n", *(stack + i) );
```

This causes the value of i to be decremented after it is compared to zero but before it is used in the printf statement. Thus, if the initial value of i is three, the values *(stack+2), *(stack+1), and *(stack+0) are printed. They correspond to stack[2], stack[1], and stack[0]. Alternately, you can write the printstack function as shown in Listing 6-14.

By storing the source code of the stack functions in a file called stack.c, the functions can be included in any program that requires them. This is done with a preprocessor #include statement.

Program Listing 6-15 exercises the stack functions. The program prompts with a * and reads the commands pop, push, print, and stop. The print command causes the contents of the stack to be printed (top to bottom). The pop command causes the top most stack element to be printed and removed from the stack. The push command takes an argument. It is entered as:

```
*push   1235
```

in which case the integer 1235 is pushed onto the stack. The stop command causes the program to exit.

The functions strcmp, atoi, and getword, which were written in Chapter 5, are used in the program. The stack functions and getword are included in the program with a

Listing 6-14. Alternate verion of Printstack.

```
printstack()  {

        int i;
        putchar('\n');
        i = stacksize();
        while(i-- > 0 )
                printf("%d\n", stack[i]);


}
```

Listing 6-15. A program to test the stack functions.

```
    #define TRUE    1
    #define FALSE   0

    #include <stdio.h>

    #include "getword.c"
    #include "stack.c"

    #define isdigit(c)   ( (c) >= '0' && (c) <= '9' ? TRUE : FALSE  )

    isinteger(sp)  char *sp; {   /* Verify that the string pointed to by
                                    sp contains only digits   */
         char *s;

         for(s = sp; *s != '\0';  s++ )
                if( !isdigit( *s )  )
                        return(FALSE);

         return(TRUE);
    }


    /* Symbolic constants to represent commands */

    #define UNKNOWN   0
    #define PRINT     1
    #define POP       2
    #define PUSH      3
    #define STOP      4

    command(s)  char *s;  {            /*  Find out which command was given */
            if(strcmp(s, "push") == 0 )
                    return(PUSH);
            if(strcmp(s, "print") == 0 )
                    return(PRINT);
            if(strcmp(s, "pop") == 0 )
                    return(POP);
            if(strcmp(s, "stop") == 0 )
                    return(STOP);
            return(UNKNOWN);

    }



    #define PROMPT    "\n*"
    #define STRINGSIZE  10

    main()  {

            char string[STRINGSIZE];
            int com;

            printf("Play with the stack functions. Enter commands:\n");
            printf("\t push nnn   pop   print  stop\n");
            printf("----------------------------------------------------\n\n");

            for(;;)  {
                    printf("%s", PROMPT);
```

```
                /* Get the command */
                getword(string, STRINGSIZE);
                if( (com = command(string) ) == STOP )
                        break;
                switch(com)  {

                        case PRINT:
                                printstack();
                                break;

                        case PUSH:
                                /* Get the digits to push */
                                getword(string, STRINGSIZE);

                                /* Make sure only digits were entered */
                                if( isinteger(string) )
                                        push( atoi(string) );
                                else
                                        printf(" Can't push %s\n", string);
                                break;

                        case POP:
                                printf("\n %d \n", pop() );
                                break;

                        default:
                                printf("\nUNKNOWN command %s\n", string);
                                break;

                };   /* This semicolon terminates switch statement */
        }   /* End of for loop */

}   /* End of main */
```

Listing 6-15 (continued)

#include preprocessor statement. The program assumes that atoi and strcmp are automatically available on your system. If that's not true on your system, you need to include these functions.

MORE ON PRINTF

In Chapter 2 you learned a method for printing character arrays. Remember that if string1 is an array of characters, say,

```
char string1[] = "a string of chars";
```

then the string is printed using the %s format, as:

```
printf("%s", string1);
```

We stressed at that time that only the name of the array is used. That is:

```
printf("%s", string1[0]);   /* WRONG*/
```

is not correct. You now know that an array name is a pointer to the beginning of the array. Now you can learn more about the %s conversion specification of printf.

When %s is used with printf, the corresponding argument must be a pointer to a null terminated string of characters. When a character array contains a string, the array name satisfies these properties. However, any legitimate pointer can be used. It need not be an array name. For example, in Listing 6-16, both printf statements cause the characters "Sample string" to be printed.

We have always used a literal string to specify the format information. For example, in:

```
printf("%d\n", i);
```

the "%d\n" is a literal string. Since printf is a function, arguments are passed to printf just as they are passed to other functions. Hence, in this example printf actually receives a pointer to the string "%d\n".

Rather than writing literal strings for conversion specifications you can use pointers to strings. Consider Listing 6-17. It prints a table of the first 99 integers and their reciprocals. The printf format information is specified by the expression:

```
i%10==0 ? doubsp:singsp
```

The value of this expression is a pointer to a character string. If i%10==0 is true, the pointer doubsp is passed to printf, otherwise singsp is passed. Since i%10==0 is true when i equals 10, 20,30, . . ., the effect of the statement is to double space every 10 lines.

Listing 6-16. Printf.

```
#include <stdio.h>

char string[] = "Sample string";

main()  {

        char *sp;
        printf("%s\n", string);  /* array name */
        sp = string;
        printf("%s\n", sp);  /* pointer */

}
```

Listing 6-17. Pointers to strings.

```
#include <stdio.h>

char *singsp = "%d       %f \n";
char *doubsp = "%d       %f \n\n";

main()   (

        int i;
        float recip;
        for(i = 1; i < 100; i++)   (

                recip = 1.0/i;
                printf(i%10 == 0   ?   doubsp:singsp, i, recip);

        )

)
```

SCANF

Scanf is the input analog of printf. The syntax of scanf is:

```
scanf(format, ptr_arg1, ptr_arg2,...)
```

Scanf reads characters from the standard input performing the conversions specified by format. The converted input is stored in the memory locations pointed to by the pointer arguments (ptr_arg1, ptr_arg2,...).

Format is a string containing the familiar conversion specifiers: %d for integer, %c for character, %s for string, %ld for long integer, etc., Examine program Listing 6-18, which illustrates the use of scanf. Note the different methods used to supply pointers for the arguments. To read integers the program uses:

```
scanf("%d", &num[i]);
```

For longs, it uses:

```
scanf("%ld", bufp);
```

and for strings, it uses:

```
scanf("%s", text);
```

Each of the expressions &num[i], bufp, and text is a pointer. Run this program on your system. When the program prompts you to enter an integer, experiment by typing several integers separated by spaces on the same line. Scanf will be discussed in detail in Chapter 8.

Listing 6-18. An example of Scanf use.

```c
#include <stdio.h>

main() {

    /*  Examples of using scanf */

    int num[5];
    long bignum[5];
    long *bigp;
    char text[81];

    int i,j;

    printf("Enter 5 integers\n");
    for(i = 0; i <5; i++)
            scanf("%d", &num[i]);
    printf("The numbers you entered are:\n");
            for(i = 0; i<5; i++)  printf("%d\n", num[i]);

    printf("Enter 5 longs\n");
    for(bigp = bignum; bigp <bignum + 5 ; bigp++  )
            scanf("%ld", bigp );

    printf("The longs you entered are:\n");
    for(i = 0; i < 5; i++)
            printf("%ld\n", bignum[i] );

    printf("Enter a string\n");
    scanf("%s", text);
    printf("\nThe string you entered is:\n\n");
    printf("%s\n", text);

}
```

MULTIDIMENSIONAL ARRAYS

All the arrays you've seen so far have been one dimensional. That is, when an array such as:

```
int number[10];
```

is defined, we can access any element of the array by using one index value, for instance, number[i] or number[7].

Consider the case of a multidimensional array. A two-dimensional array is easily viewed as a table. Figure 6-8 shows four temperature readings in three cities. The data are organized as a table with three rows and four columns. You can store this data in three separate arrays, as:

```
int tempny[4] = {70,82,75,60}; /*NYs data*/
int templa[4] = {78,83,65,60}; /*LAs data*/
int tempsf[4] = {58,65,57,50}; /*SFs data*/
```

Using this data organization you can see if LA's temperature reached 90 degrees by writing:

```
for(i=0; i<4; i++)
    if(templa[i] >=90) {
        printf("LA Broke 90 degrees\n");
        break;

    }
```

Similarly, if ip has been defined as an integer pointer, you can write:

```
for(ip=templa; ip<templa +4; ip++)
    if(*ip >= 90) {
```

	Time			
	8am	Noon	8pm	Midnight
NY	70	82	75	60
LA	78	83	65	60
SF	58	65	57	50

Fig. 6-8. Temperature readings in farenheit for three cities.

169

```
        printf("LA Broke 90 degrees\n");
        break;
    }
```

Alternately you can define a two-dimensional array to hold the temperature readings with a declaration in the following form:

```
int temps[3][4];
```

You can think of this declaration as defining a table with three rows and four columns. This declaration defines 12 storage locations for integers. They are stored contiguously in memory in row order. When you think of the two dimensional array as a table, you can reference the individual elements are temps[0][0], temps[0] [1],...,temps[2] [3]. As with one dimensional arrays, indexing starts with zero. For an example, if the temperature data for LA is in the table's second row (the row index 1), the above program fragment would look like this:

```
for(i = 0; i<4; i++)
    if(temps[1][i] >= 90)  {
        printf("LA Broke 90 degrees\n");
        break;
    }
```

Actually, the declaration:

```
int temps[3][4];
```

defines an array with three elements. Each element is a row of the table. Thus, each element is itself an array with four elements.

The notion of defining an "array of arrays," is why C uses the notation temps[3] [4] rather than the commonly used notation temps[3,4]. What is meant by saying that:

```
int temps[3][4];
```

defines an array of three elements is that temps[0], temps[1], and temps[2] are automatically initialized as pointers to their respective rows. That is, temps[0] is a pointer to temps[0] [0], temps[1] is a pointer to temps[1] [0], and temps[2] is a pointer to temps[2] [0]. Further, the word temps (without brackets), is a pointer to temps[0]. Temps is the first example you have seen of a "pointer to a pointer." This concept is discussed later. Using pointer notation, if ip is an integer pointer, the above program fragment can be written like this:

```
for(ip=temps[1]; ip < temps[1] + 4; ip++)
    if( *ip >= 90)  {
            printf("LA Broke 90 degrees\n");
            break;
    }
```

In summary, when the two dimensional array:

```
int temps[3][4];
```

is defined, three groups of objects are actually defined:

- Twelve integer variables known as temps[0] [0], temps[0] [1],...,temps[2] [3]
- Three pointers to integers known as temps[0], temps[1], and temps[2]
- And one pointer to a pointer to an integer known as temps.

Figure 6-9 shows these relationships. In the figure, we have initialized the array to hold the data of Fig. 6-8.

Arrays of more than two dimensions can be defined. For example:

```
float space[10][10][10];
```

defines 1000 float variables. They are known as space[0] [0] [0], space[0] [0] [1], and so on. Furthermore, 100 pointers to float (space[0] [0],...space[9] [9]), ten pointers to pointers to float (space[0],...space[9]), and one pointer to pointer to pointer to float (space) are also defined.

When multidimensional arrays are passed to functions only the first dimension (the row dimension) can be left unspecified. For example, in:

```
process(table,n)
        int table[][10];
        int n;
        {
            /*function to process a table*/
        }
```

a two dimensional array is passed to the function process. It is

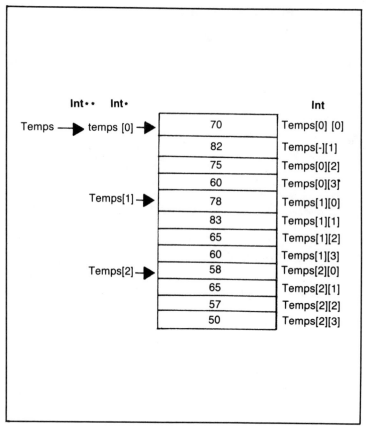

Int•• Int•		Int
Temps → temps [0] →	70	Temps[0] [0]
	82	Temps[-][1]
	75	Temps[0][2]
	60	Temps[0][3]
Temps[1] →	78	Temps[1][0]
	83	Temps[1][1]
	65	Temps[1][2]
	60	Temps[1][3]
Temps[2] →	58	Temps[2][0]
	65	Temps[2][1]
	57	Temps[2][2]
	50	Temps[2][3]

Fig. 6-9. Data and pointer relationships from the declaration:
PICK UP ART HERE

necessary to specify how many columns are in the table, but it is not necessary to specify the number of rows. As with one dimensional arrays, a pointer to the beginning of the table will be passed.

In a like manner, consider:

```
aprocess(arr_table,n)

        int arr_table[] [10] [10];
        int n;

        (

                /* function to process an array

        )
```

For the three dimensional arr_table, it is necessary to specify the size of the last two dimensions.

INITIALIZING ARRAYS

When an array external to all functions is defined it can be initialized by following the array declaration with a brace-enclosed list of initializers. For instance:

```
int counts[10] = {0,1,2,3,4,5,6,7,8,9};

main() {



    .
    .
    .



}
```

initializes counts[0] to 0, counts[1] to 1, etc. If all initializers are present the dimension of the array need not be specified; so:

```
int counts[] = {0,1,2,3,4,5,6,7,8,9};

main() {



    .
    .
    .



}
```

is equivalent to the previous declaration.

Within a function, automatic arrays may not be initialized. To write:

```
main() {

    /* WRONG */

    int counts[] = {0,1,2,3,4,5,6,7,8,9};

}
```

is not correct since in this example the array counts is automatic.

If it is necessary to initialize an array that is local to a function, the array must be defined as static. So:

```
main() {

    static int counts[] = {0,1,2,3,4,5,6,7,7,8,9};

        .
        .
        .

    {
```

}

will correctly initialize the array.

Character arrays can be initialized with strings, as in:

```
char greeting[] = "hello";
```

Or they can be initialized with character constants, as in:

```
char greeting[]= {'h','e','l','l','o','\0'};
```

Note that with the latter method you must explicitly supply the end-of-string marker.

When multidimensional arrays are initialized, they are initialized by rows. Each row of initializers is enclosed in brackets. For example:

```
int table[][] = {

        {0,0},   /*data for first row*/
        {1,1},   /*data for second row*/
        {2,2}    /*data for third row*/

};
```

sets table[0] [0] and table[0] [1] to 0, table[1] [0] and table[1] [1] to 1, and table[2] [0] and table[2] [1] to 2. When some initializers are not present dimensions must be specified. Uninitialized array elements are set to zero. For example:

```
int table[5] [5] = {

        {0,1,2,3,4},
        {10,11,12,13,14},
        {20,21},
```

initializes the first row of the table with the integers 0–4, and the second row of the table with the integers 10–14. In the third row only the first two columns (table[2] [0] and table[2] [1]) are initialized. The remainder of that row and rows four and five are initialized to zero. Multidimensional arrays, like their one dimensional counterparts, must be either external to all functions or static to be initialized.

FUNCTIONS THAT RETURN POINTERS

Functions are allowed to return pointers. For instance, consider the definition of the function *strchr*. Strchr searches a string looking for the occurrence of a character. If the character is there, strchr returns a pointer to it (see Listing 6-19). The "char ★" before the function name says "strchr" is a function that returns a pointer to a character. This is an extension of the discussion in Chapter 3.

As a matter of typing style, you can vary the amount of white space between the components of this declaration. For example:

```
char * strchr(s,c)
```

or

```
char *strchr(s,c)
```

or:

```
char *
strchr(s,c)
```

are all valid.

Functions returning pointers to other types are declared analogously. For instance, a function definition beginning:

```
int *iflip()
```

returns a pointer to an integer, and:

```
float * iflop()
```

returns a pointer to a float.

Listing 6-19. The function Strchr.

```
    char * strchr(s,c)
            char s[];
            char c;
    {   /* Return pointer to c if c is in s.  Otherwise, return NULL */

            register char *sp;

            for(sp = s;  *sp; sp++)
                    if(*sp == c)
                            return(sp);

            return(NULL);

    }
```

175

ARRAYS OF POINTERS

You have seen declarations of the form:

```
char *day;
```

This declaration defines the variable day as a pointer to a character. As of yet, day doesn't point to anything; however, an expression of the form:

```
day = "Monday";
```

does point it to something. It directs the compiler to store the string "Monday" (terminated by \0) somewhere in memory and to put the string's address into the variable day.

The declaration:

```
char *dayname[] = {

        "",
        "Monday",
        "Tuesday",
        "Wednesday",
        "Thursday",
        "Friday",
        "Saturday",
        "Sunday"

};
```

defines an array with eight elements. Each element is a pointer to a string. This is your first example of an array of pointers. The array element dayname[1] is a pointer to the string "Monday", dayname[2] is a pointer to the string "Tuesday", etc. We have set dayname[0] to point to the null string so that the numbers for legitimate day names range from 1-7.

An array of pointers is still an array, so everything stated about arrays still applies. For example, the name dayname without brackets points to dayname[0]. The elements dayname[0], dayname[1], and so on are stored contiguously in memory. Figure 6-10 graphically depicts the result of the above declaration.

The function get_day_name uses this array to convert a day number into a pointer to that day's name (Listing 6-20). There are a few things to note about this function: a) since it returns a pointer to a string, it's definition begins:

```
char *get_day_name(n)
```

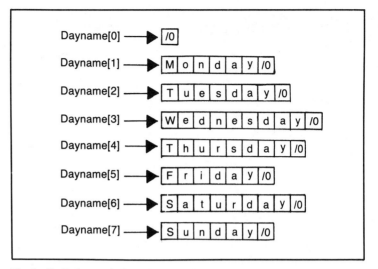

Fig. 6-10. Pointer relationships resulting from the declaration:
PICK UP ART HERE

meaning "function that returns a pointer to char"; b) within the function, the array of pointers dayname is declared as static because it is being initialized; c) if an erroneous day number is passed, get_day_name returns NULL. NULL is symbolically defined as:

```
#define NULL 0
```

Because C guarantees that a pointer to valid data will never be zero, NULL serves as a signal that an error has occurred.

Listing 6-20. Get_day_name, function.

```
        char *get_day_name(n)
               int n;
        {
               static char *dayname[] = {
                       "",
                       "Monday",
                       "Tuesday",
                       "Wednesday",
                       "Thursday",
                       "Friday",
                       "Saturday",
                       "Sunday"

               };

               return(1 <= n && n <= 7  ? dayname[n]:NULL);

        }
```

ARRAYS OF POINTERS VERSUS
TWO DIMENSIONAL ARRAYS

Arrays of pointers can be used in applications where two dimensional arrays might otherwise be used. Consider Listing 6-21, which reads words from the standard input and stores them in a two dimensional array of type char. The program uses the function getword, which was written in Chapter 5.

This program preallocates 400 bytes of memory in the array called word (20 words with 20 bytes for each word). Clearly, a good deal of the memory will not be used, because most words will be shorter than the 19 characters (remember the end-of-string marker takes one character).

An alternate approach to storage is to dynamically allocate memory for the words. You can do this by first reading the word you want to store and then requesting the exact amount of memory required to store it. Most environments that support C will supply a function to perform dynamic storage allocation. This is the function you call to request memory. Typical names for the function are alloc, malloc, and calloc. You need to review the documentation supplied with your compiler to determine the name of your storage allocation function.

To use calloc, for example, you call it as:

```
calloc(number_of_elements, element_size)
```

Listing 6-21. Two-dimensional array storage example.

```
#include <stdio.h>

/*  The file getword.c (Chapter 5) must be on your disk. */
#include "getword.c"

#define NUMBER_OF_WORDS  20
#define WORDSIZE  20

char word[NUMBER_OF_WORDS][WORDSIZE];

main()  {
        int i;

        printf("\nType text on the keyboard.\n");
        printf("The first %d words will be stored.\n\n\n", NUMBER_OF_WORDS);

        for(i = 0;  i < NUMBER_OF_WORDS;  i++)
                getword(word[i], WORDSIZE);

        printf("\n\n");
        printf("The first %d words you typed are:\n", NUMBER_OF_WORDS);
        for( i = 0; i < NUMBER_OF_WORDS;  i++)
                printf("%d>  %s\n", i+1 , word[i] );

}
```

Calloc returns a pointer to a block of unused memory large enough to hold the specified number of elements of the specified size. The pointer returned by calloc points to the type char. If sufficient memory is not available, calloc returns NULL.

With the declarations:

```
int n = 30;   char *word_pointer;
```

the function calloc is called as:

```
word_pointer = calloc(n,sizeof(char));
```

With this call, calloc returns a pointer to the beginning of 30 bytes of unused memory. If calloc cannot provide the desired amount of memory it returns NULL.

Using a storage allocation function, the above program can be rewritten according to the following storage strategy: read the word to be stored into a buffer; request the proper amount of memory to store the word; copy the buffer into the memory that was allocated. With this approach you need to keep track of the location of the memory allocated for you. This can be done with an array of pointers. The rewrite in Listing 6-22 of the previous program illustrates these ideas. It uses getword, and strcpy from Chapter 5, and calloc to allocate storage. You need to modify this program for your system if calloc is not available to you.

Though this version of the program does not use excess memory to store words, it does use some additional memory to store the array of pointers. But aside from memory use, the array of pointers approach offers other advantages. Consider the task of sorting the words. If you apply the bubblesort technique illustrated in Chapter 5 you can sort the two dimensional array with the following program fragment. (Assume the declarations int i,j,lastindex; char temp_word[WORDSIZE]; have been made):

```
for(i = 0, lastindex = NUMBER_OF_WORDS-1;
    lastindex > 0; --lastindex)
  for(j = 0; j<lastindex; j++)
    if(strcmp(word[j], word[j+1]) >0) {
          /*words are out of order*/
          strcpy(temp_word, word[j]);
          strcpy(word[j], word[j+1]);
          strcpy(word[j+1], temp_word);

    }
```

Note that when two words are found to be out of order strcpy is

Listing 6-22. An example of dynamic storage allocation.

```
#include <stdio.h>
#include "getword.c"    /*  From Chapter 5 */

/*  NOTE:
        If your system does not automatically link strcpy into your
    programs, type the version presented in Chapter 5 here */

#define NUMBER_OF_WORDS   20
char *wordp[NUMBER_OF_WORDS];   /* An array of pointers */

#define BUFSIZE  20
char buffer[BUFSIZE];

main() {

        int i,n;
        char *calloc();  /* Declare the storage allocation function */

        printf("Type text on the keyboard\n");
        printf("The first %d words will be stored\n\n", NUMBER_OF_WORDS);

        for(i = 0;  i < NUMBER_OF_WORDS;  i++)  {
                n = getword(buffer, BUFSIZE);

                /* get storage for the word + end-of-string marker */
                wordp[i] = calloc(n + 1, sizeof(char) );
                if(wordp[i] != NULL)
                        strcpy(wordp[i], buffer);
                else
                        printf("Sorry - no room to store the word\n");

        }

        printf("\n\n");
        printf("The first %d words you typed are:\n\n", NUMBER_OF_WORDS);
        for(i = 0; i < NUMBER_OF_WORDS; i++ )
                printf("%d>    %s\n", i+1, wordp[i] );

}
```

called to exchange them. This results in three character-by-character copy operations.

With the array of pointers approach, bubblesort can be applied in the following way (assume the declarations int i, j, lastindex; char *temp_wordp; char *wordp[NUMBER_OF_WORDS]; have been made):

```
for(i = 0, lastindex = NUMBER_OF_WORDS-1;
     lastindex >0; --lastindex)
     for(j = 0; j < lastindex; j++)

             if(strcmp(wordp[j], wordp[j+1]) {
                     /*words are out of order*/
                     temp_wordp = wordp[j];
```

```
wordp[j] = wordp[j+1];
wordp[j+1] = temp_wordp;

}
```

In this version only the pointers are exchanged; the strings themselves are not moved. By eliminating the character-by-character copy operations, sorting is faster. (*Note:* Still faster sorts can be obtained by using sorting techniques that are better than bubblesort. See Chapter 9, Pointers to Functions).

COMMAND LINE ARGUMENTS

You can pass arguments to programs when you execute them. Arguments are passed on the command line. An array of pointers is used by the program to retrieve arguments from the command line.

When a program is invoked, the command line looks like this:

```
A> prog
```

The A> in this example represents the operating system prompt, and prog is the name of the program. When a program is invoked, as:

```
A> prog jim bill
```

the character strings jim and bill are considered arguments for the program. The mechanism by which the program accesses its arguments is through an array of pointers.

Every program that you've seen so far in this book has had a main function with no formal parameters. Main has always appeared as:

```
main() {
      .
      .
      .
}
```

When command line arguments are to be passed to a program the definition of main begins as follows:

```
main(argc,argv)
     int argc;
```

```
char *argv[]; {
    .
    .
    .

}
```

When execution of main begins the integer variable argc will equal the number of command line arguments present. The name of the program is counted as one argument, so argc is at least one. In our example:

```
A> prog jim bill
```

argc equals three.

Each element in the pointer array argv points to a command line argument. Setting aside the program name for a moment, argv[1] will point to the first command line argument, argv[2] the second command line argument, ..., argv[argc-1] points to the last command line argument. In the example above, argv[1] points to the string jim, and argv[2] points to the string bill.

As you may have guessed, argv[0] is the pointer for the program name. Under UNIX, argv[0] does in fact point to the program's name. However, as of this writing, this is not true for C compilers running under CP/M or MS-DOS. These operating systems do not keep track of a program's name. Hence, argv[0] points to either a null string or garbage. Figure 6-11 illustrates this example.

As a simple example, Listing 6-23 prints its command line arguments. The names argc and argv are conventional, not

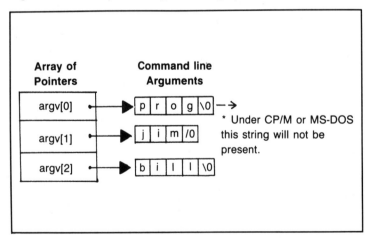

Fig. 6-11. Command Line Arguments.

182

Listing 6-23. Printing command line arguments.

```
#include <stdio.h>

main(argc,argv)
        int argc;
        char *argv[];   (

        int i;

        /* print command line arguments, ignore argv[0] */
        for(i = 1; i < argc; i++)
                printf("%s\n", argv[i]);

}
```

required; any names can be used. We will return to the topic of command line arguments in the next section and present several examples of programs using command line arguments in Chapter 8.

★ POINTERS TO POINTERS

Consider an integer variable and a pointer to an integer declared as follows:

```
int i = 10;
int *p;
```

Suppose you apply the address-of operator to both i and p. For instance:

```
p = &i;   /* make p point to i */
q = &p;   /* can you do this? */
```

The above declarations have declared two objects—an integer i and a pointer to an integer p. The assignment statements have introduced q, another variable. Figure 6-12 shows the relationship between i, p, and q. For the relationships shown in Fig. 6-12 to be correct, the variables must be declared as:

```
int i=10, *p, **q;
```

The figure shows that q is a pointer to a pointer. In other words, i's address is stored in the variable p, and p's address is stored in the variable q. Hence, if you start at q you must go through two levels of indirection to fetch the value of i. So the value of i is 10, the value of ★p is 10, and the value of ★★q is 10. The notation ★★q means "apply the indirection operator to q

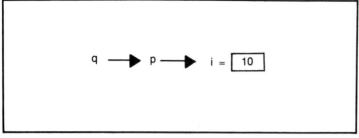

Fig. 6-12. Pointer relationship defined by:

twice.'' As the declaration suggests, the objects denoted by i, ★p, and ★★q are all integers. With the relationship of Fig. 6-11 and the variable i initialized to 10, the expressions:

```
i + 1
*p + 1
**q + 1
```

all denote the addition of two integers. Each expression has the value 11.

C does not explicitly limit the number of levels of indirection that can be used. A declaration such as:

```
int ***p;
```

means ★★★p is an integer, ★★p is a pointer to an integer, ★p is a pointer to a pointer to an integer, and p is a pointer to a pointer to a pointer to an integer.

You have seen that a C program can retrieve command line arguments when the function main begins, as:

```
main(argc,argv)
    int argc;
    char *argv[];   /* Method 1 */
```

A program can also retrieve command line arguments when main begins as:

```
main(argc,argv)

    int argc;
    char **argv;   /* Method 2 */
```

The first method above specifies that an array of pointers called argv[ ] will be passed to main. You know that C doesn't actually pass an entire array; what is passed is a pointer to the beginning

Listing 6-24. Another method of printing command line arguments.

```
#include <stdio.h>

main(argc,argv)
        int argc;
        char **argv;   {

        for(++argv;  --argc;  ++argv)
                printf("%s\n", *argv);

}
```

of the array. So in this case what is passed is a pointer to a pointer. Hence, the declaration shown in the second method:

char **argv;.

The program in the last section which prints its arguments can also be written like Listing 6-24. When this program is executed argv initially points to argv[0]. In the initialization portion of the for loop the expression ++argv makes it point to argv[1]. Thus, the string pointed to by argv[0] is not printed.

In the test portion of the for loop argc is decremented using prefix notation (--agrc). This decrements argc prior to testing it and compensates for the fact that the string pointed to by argv[0] is counted as an argument.

In the printf statement, since argv is a pointer to a pointer to a string, *argv is a pointer to a string. That is what printf expects with the %s format. Finally, the increment expression of the for loop (++argv) makes argv point to the next argument.

In this chapter the basic concepts of pointers have been discussed. You should now be able to read and write pointer expressions in C programs.

In the chapters that follow additional information on pointer use will be addressed. Notably, Chapter 7 introduces pointers to structures and Chapter 9 addresses pointers to functions.

EXERCISES

1. Describe what Listing 6-25 will print:

Listing 6-25. Exercise 1.

```
#include <stdio.h>

char alpha[] = "abcdefghijklmnopqrstuvwxyz";

main()  {
        char *alpha_ptr;
```

185

```
        alpha_ptr = alpha;
        while(*alpha_ptr)  {
                printf("%s\n", alpha_ptr);
                alpha_ptr++;

        }
```

2. Compile, link, and execute the program in exercise 1. Was your description of its output correct?

3. The intent of the following function (Listing 6-26) is to write a string to the standard output:

Listing 6-26. Exercise 3.

```
        puts(s)  char *s;  {
                char *sp;

                sp = s;
                while(*sp++ != '\0')
                        putchar(*sp);

        }
```

Will this function work correctly? If not, why?

4. Pointer versions of programs often run faster than non-pointer versions. Devise a timing experiment on your system to test the relative speed of a pointer version versus a non-pointer version of a program.

5. Using the stack functions shown on page 162, what will be printed by the statement:

```
printf("%d", push(pop()));
```

How will the execution of this statement affect the elements on the stack?

6. Add a command called *top* to the program which exercises the stack functions (page 164). The top command should print the top-most stack element without removing it from the stack.

7. Write a main function to test get_day_name. The main function prompts for numbers to be entered and prints the corresponding day's name. Use scanf to perform input.

Chapter 7

Structures

In everyday spoken language you can easily group related pieces of information. For example, under the heading "car," you can speak of the car's radio, the car's tires, the car's battery, the car's engine, and so on.

In C, structures are used to group related items of information. Structures group related variables and arrays together under a structure name. As an example of the syntax, consider a structure named *car*, which groups the related items from the spoken language analogy above:

```
struct {
    int tires;
    int radio;
    int battery;
    int engine;
} car;
```

This declaration defines a structure named car. The related items can now be referenced in a C program as car.tires, car.radio, car.battery, and car.engine. Each reference refers to an int variable.

In this chapter, you will explore the use of structures.

DECLARING STRUCTURES

Consider the kind of information that would be stored for one person in a mailing list. There is the name, address, city, state, zipcode. For any person on the list this information is related. For instance, for a person named Joe the information would represent Joe's name, Joe's address, Joe's zipcode, and so on.

You can preserve the grouping of information by using a C structure. A structure declaration has the following form:

```
struct {

    /* Variables of the structure */

} struct_name;
```

The declaration begins with the keyword struct. Then, enclosed in brackets are declarations of all of the related variables that are part of the structure. Finally there is the name of the structure and a semicolon terminator.

As an example, the declaration:

```
struct {
    char first_name[NAMESIZE];
    char last_name[NAMESIZE];
    char address[ADDRSIZE];
    char city[NAMESIZE];
    char state[3];
    long zipcode;
} mail;
```

defines a structure named mail. The structure mail contains six related variables; five character arrays and a long int. These related variables are called members of the structure.

The individual members of the structure are accessed by using the structure member operator. It is denoted by a period (.). The syntax for this operator's use is:

```
structure_name.member_name
```

For instance:

`mail.first_name[0]` refers to the zero-th element of the first_name array

`mail.zipcode` refers to the long int zipcode

For the arrays in the structure mail, everything stated about stated about arrays in Chapter 6 is still true, so:

`mail.first_name`   is a pointer to mail.first_name[0]

`mail.address`   is a pointer to mail.address[0]

arrays in Chapter 6 is valid, so:

As an example of how structure members are accessed in a program, Listing 7-1 fills the above structure with information, then prints the structure's contents. Scanf is used as the input function.

When a variable is declared within a structure its name will not conflict with variables declared outside the structure. For instance, consider the following declarations:

```
int count;
struct {
     int count;
     char item;
} word;
```

The integer variable word.count within the structure does not have a name conflict with the integer variable count outside the structure. They are two different variables. The compiler can tell which you are referring to by the presence or absence of the structure name.

It also is permissible to name a structure with the same name as one of its members. For example, consider:

```
struct {
     char *name;
     int index;
} index;
```

In this example index is the name of a structure, index.index is an integer variable within the structure.

STRUCTURE TAGS AND TEMPLATES

Because structures can have a long list of members, there is an alternate way to declare them. You can create a template of what members are in the structure and then use the template in subsequent declarations. This style of declaration has the following form:

```
struct  struct_tag {
     /* Variables of the structure*/
};
```

189

Listing 7-1. Acessing structure numbers.

```c
#include <stdio.h>

#define NAMESIZE 20
#define ADDRSIZE 30

struct {
        char first_name[NAMESIZE];
        char last_name[NAMESIZE];
        char address[ADDRSIZE];
        char city[NAMESIZE];
        char state[3];
        long zipcode;
} mail;

fill_mail()
{
        /* Fill the mail structure with information */

        printf("Enter a mail record\n");
        printf("First name: ");
        scanf("%s", mail.first_name);
        printf("Last name: ");
        scanf("%s", mail.last_name);
        printf("Address: ");
        scanf("%s", mail.address);
        printf("City: ");
        scanf("%s", mail.city);
        printf("State: ");
        scanf("%s", mail.state);
        printf("Zipcode: ");
        scanf("%ld",&mail.zipcode);
}

print_mail()
{
        /* Print the contents of the mail struct */

        printf("%s ",    mail.first_name);
        printf("%s\n",    mail.last_name);
        printf("%s\n",  mail.address);
        printf("%s\n",  mail.city);
        printf("%s   ", mail.state);
        printf("%ld\n", mail.zipcode);

}

main() {
        fill_mail();
        print_mail();
}
```

For example, to make a template for the information of the structure mail, you can write:

```
struct list_element {

    char first_name[NAMESIZE];
    char last_name[NAMESIZE];
    char address[ADDRSIZE];
    char city[NAMESIZE];
    char state[3];
    long zipcode;
};
```

This declaration defines a structure tag called list_element. This tag becomes a shorthand notation for the complete list of structure elements. You can now define structures containing the variables shown in the list element template as follows:

```
struct list_element mail;
```

This declaration defines the variables mail.first_name, mail.last_name, etc. Further, the declaration:

```
struct list_element mail, christmas;
```

defines two structures with the members shown in the list element template. References to christmas.zipcode, or mail.zipcode refer to the long int in each of the structures.

Defining a structure template is somewhat like defining a new type for variables. That is, just as you declare:

```
int x,y,z;
```

you can now declare:

```
struct list_element x,y,z;
```

The "struct list_element" serves like a type name for the variables x,y, and z.

Notice that when only a structure template is defined, no memory is set aside for variables. For example, the declaration:

```
struct date {
    int month;
    int day;
    int year;

};
```

does not cause any memory locations to be set aside for date, month, day, or year. So, attempting to reference:

```
date.month   /*WRONG*/
```

is not correct. Date is not a variable. It is a structure tag that serves as a shorthand notation to define variables.

A subsequent definition of the form:

```
struct date today;
```

does define variables. Today is a variable that refers to a struct, today.month is an int variable, etc.

The two steps of defining a structure template and defining an actual structure containing the variables of the template can be combined into one step as follows:

```
struct date {
int month;
int day;
int year;

} birth, death;
```

In this declaration, the structure tag date is defined. Date now represents a shorthand to declare a structure with the integer variables month, day, and year. Also, two actual structures—birth and death—are defined. So references of the form:

```
birth.day
birth.month
birth.year
```

refer to integers in the birth structure. Similarly, death.day, death.month, and death.year refer to integers in the death structure. Any subsequent need to define structures containing the date information can be handled by a declaration like:

```
struct date anniversary, retirement;
```

A structure can be initialized by writing a bracket-enclosed list of initializers after the structure name. For example:

```
struct {

    int day;
    int month;
```

```
        int year;

    } birth = (17,5,1910);
```

initializes birth.day to 17, birth.month to 5, and birth.year to 1910.

STRUCTURES IN STRUCTURES

Structures can be embedded inside of other structures. For example, the declaration:

```
struct project {

    struct date start;
    struct date finish;
    float budget;
    float cost;
    float profit;

} x,y;
```

defines a structure template called project. Two actual project structures—x and y—are also declared. References of the form x.budget, or y.cost refer to float variables within the x and y project structures, respectively.

To reference members of the start date structure within x, the structure operator (.) is applied twice. Hence, a reference looks like this:

```
x.start.day
x.start.month
x.start.year
```

The same logic of repeatedly using the (.) operator applies when structures are nested to deeper levels. For example, with the declaration:

```
struct {

    struct project electrical;
    struct project foundation;
    struct project walls;
    struct project phones;
    struct project finish;

} building;
```

building.phones.budget refers to a float variable, and building. electrical.start.month refers to an int variable.

You cannot embed a structure within itself. For example:

```
struct project {

        struct date start;
        struct date finish;
        float budget;
        struct project subcontract;   /* ILLEGAL*/

    } job;
```

is illegal because the project template contains an occurrence of itself.

ARRAYS OF STRUCTURES

Earlier we defined a structure template with the tag list_element. For ease of reference, it is reproduced here:

```
struct list_element {

        char first_name[NAMESIZE];
        char last_name[NAMESIZE];
        char address[ADDRSIZE];
        char city[NAMESIZE];
        char state[3];
        long zipcode;
    };
```

We now use this template to define an array. Each element of the array is a structure:

```
#define LISTSIZE      500
struct list_element mail[LISTSIZE];
```

This declaration defines an array of structures (mail[0], mail[1], ... ,mail[LISTSIZE-1]). Each of the structures has the members first_name, last_name, address, etc. Figure 7-1 depicts the result of this declaration.

The structure operator is applied as before, so:

mail[0].first_name	pointer to first_name[0] in mail[0]
mail[1].first_name	pointer to first_name[0] in mail[1]
.	
.	
.	
mail[5].zipcode	zipcode in mail[5]

refer to various members of various structures.

194

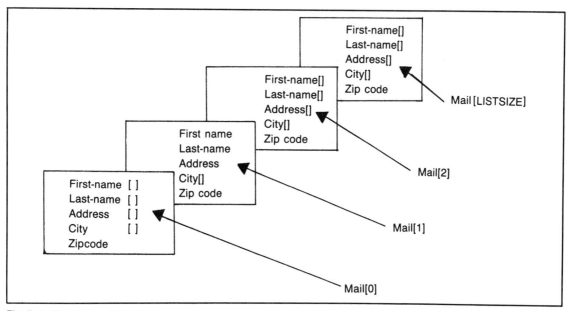

Fig. 7-1. The Array of Mail Structures.

Structure arrays can be initialized by following the array name by an equal sign and a brace-enclosed list of initializers. The initializers for each structure are also enclosed in braces and separated by commas. For example, the declaration:

```
struct {

     int num;
     char * name;

} day[] = {

     {0, "Illegal"},        /* data for struct day[0] */
     {1, "Monday"},         /* data for struct day[1] */
     {2, "Tuesday"},
     {3, "Wednesday"},
     {4, "Thursday"},
     {5, "Friday"},
     {6, "Saturday"},
     {7, "Sunday"}          /* data for struct day[7] */

};
```

defines an array of structures named day. For an integer j, day[j].num is the day's number, and day[j].name is a pointer to a character string that contains the day's name. We have associated the name "Illegal" with the integer 0 so that the numbers

195

1–7 may be used to index the array. We did not explicitly state the size of the array; when all initializers are present, the C compiler will count them and size the array accordingly.

Using a slight variant of this structure definition, we define a function called daynum which takes a day name as an argument, and returns the corresponding day number (see Listing 7-2).

Listing 7-2. The Daynum function.

```
#define tolower(c)  ( 'A' <= (c) && (c) <= 'Z' ) ? (c) + 32 : (c)
convert_to_lower(out_name, in_name )
        char out_name[], in_name[];
        /* convert the name to lower case */
{
        int i;
        for(i=0; in_name[i] != '\0' ; i++ )
                out_name[i] = tolower( in_name[i] );
        out_name[i] = '\0';    /* terminate the string */
}

/* define an array of structs which relate
   day names to day numbers  */
struct {
        int num;
        char *name;
} days[] = {
        { 5, "friday"},
        { 1, "monday"},
        { 6, "saturday"},
        { 7, "sunday"},
        { 4, "thursday"},
        { 2, "tuesday"},
        { 3, "wednesday"}
};
#define MAXNAME 15
daynum( name)  char * name;
{
        /* Return the day number ( 1 for Monday ... 7 for Sunday ) associated
           with name.  Return 0 if name is not a day name */

        char lowname[MAXNAME];
        int i;
        int match_status;

        convert_to_lower(lowname, name);

        for( i=0; i<7; i++ ) {
                match_status = strcmp(lowname, days[i].name);
                if ( match_status == 0 )  /* a match */
                        return( days[i].num );
                if (match_status < 0 )    /* no match is possible */
                        return(0);
        }
        /* searched the entire array of structs without a match */
        return(0);
}
```

```
main() {

    /* a main function to test daynum */

    int i,j;
    char name[MAXNAME];

    printf("Enter 10 names for testing\n");
    for(i=0; i<10 ; i++ ) {
        printf("Enter a name ");
        scanf("%s", name);
        j = daynum( name );
        printf("The name %s produced the number %d\n", name, j );
    }
}
```

In daynum, the candidate name is converted to lowercase so the function is insensitive to the case of its argument. In the for loop, we are calling strcmp. The call is stated as:

match_status=strcmp(lowname, days[i].name)

Since strcmp expects pointers, we reference the array as days[i].name. This is the name of an array of type char, so it serves as a pointer to the string. Match_status is used to record the result of the comparison. Since the array was initialized in alphabetical order, when:

$$match\_status < 0$$

is true, there is no need to search the array further.

POINTERS TO STRUCTURES

You have seen how to use the structure member operator (.) . Another operator that can be applied to a structure is the address-of operator (&). When the address-of operator is applied to a structure the result is the address of the structure. As before, applying the & operator yields a pointer.

For example, consider the structure template:

```
struct date {
    /* a template for a date structure */
    int month;
    int day;
    int year;
};
```

The declaration:

```
struct date birth, death, *b, *d;
```

197

defines two date structures (birth and death) and two pointers to date structures (b and d). Though the variables b and d are pointers to structures, this declaration does not point them at anything. Using the address-of operator, you can write statements like:

```
b = &birth;
d = &death;
```

which cause b to point to the birth structure and d to point to the death structure. Alternatively, you can take care of initializing the pointers while declaring them like this:

```
struct date birth, death;
struct date *b = &birth, *d = &death;
```

Figure 7-2 depicts this relationship.

C provides the -> operator to access members of structures via pointers. (The symbol -> is typed by using the minus sign followed by the greater than sign.) For example, with the pointer b pointing to the birth structure, the members of the birth structure can be accessed as:

```
b->day
b->month
b->year
```

Each of these refers to an integer variable.

The indirection operator (*) can also be used to access a member of a structure via a pointer to it. Using this operator, the

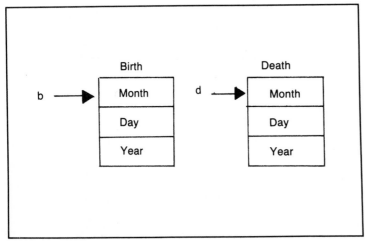

Fig. 7-2. Variable Relationship From: struct date birth, death; and struct * b = &birth, *d = &death;.

198

same three integers would be accessed as:

```
(*b).day
(*b).month
(*b).year
```

With this notation the parentheses are necessary. Without them
★b.day is interpreted by the compiler as ★(b.day) since the
precedence of the structure member operator is higher than the
precedence of the indirection operator. Table 7–1 updates the
operator precedence table to include the structure operators (->
and .). Though b->day and (★b).day have the same meaning,
the former notation is more commonly used. Note that the ->
operator is not being applied to a structure, but to a pointer to a
structure.

**Table 7–1. Precedence of the Arithmetic,
Relational, Pointer, And Structure Operators.**

Operator Use	Operator Symbol	Associativity
function calls array references struct member struct member via pointer	() [] . ->	Left To Right
address-of indirection unary minus increment, decrement cast, sizeof negation	& * − ++ −− (type) sizeof !	Right To Left
multiply, divide modulus	* / %	Left To Right
add, subtract	+−	Left To Right
relational	< <= > >=	Left To Right
equality, inequality	== !=	Left To Right
logical connective and	&&	Left To Right
logical connective or	||	Left To Right
conditional	?:	Right To Left
assignment	= += −= *= /= %=	Right To Left
sequential execution	,	Left To Right

Note: *Operators between horizontal bars have same precedence and
associativity. Top of table is the highest precedence operators.*

the number returned is the current memory address of the variable following the & sign (not the value of the variable as would be normal)

The number returned is the value at the address found by using the given variable as the address of the number to be found

199

Assigning the value of one pointer to another is a technique you used in Chapter 6. This technique remains valid when pointers to structures are used. For instance, given the declarations:

```
struct date birth, death;
struct date *b = &birth, *d = &death;
```

the statement:

```
d = b;
```

causes d to point to the birth structure.

The declarations:

```
struct date attend[12];
struct date *ap = attend;
```

first define an array of 12 structures. As with arrays of the basic types, the name attend is a pointer to attend[0]. The second declaration defines ap as a pointer to a structure of type date, and initializes ap to hold the address of attend[0]. A statement of the form:

```
ap = &attend[5];
```

makes ap point to attend[5], as does the statement:

```
ap = attend+5;
```

The latter statement is, once again, address arithmetic. Just as address arithmetic was used on arrays of the basic types, it can be used on arrays of structures.

Program Listing 7-3 illustrates some of the basic notation used when accessing structure members within the array attend. Note that when ap points to an element of the array attend, ap++ makes ap point to the next array element. Because each element of the array is a structure, the address arithmetic marches the pointer from structure to structure.

PASSING STRUCTURE DATA TO FUNCTIONS

When information is contained within a structure it is sometimes desirable to pass this information to a function. For example, consider the structure:

```
struct date {
        int month;
        int day;
        int year;
} today;
```

200

Listing 7-3. Accesing members of an array of structures.

```c
#include <stdio.h>

struct date  {
        int day;
        int month;
        int year;
};

struct date attend[12];

main()  {

        struct date *ap;

        int start_day = 1;
        int start_month = 1;
        int start_year = 1984;

        /* initialize the array attend */

        for(ap = attend; ap < attend+12; ap++)  {
                ap -> day = start_day++;
                ap -> month = start_month++;
                ap -> year = start_year++;
        }

        /* Print the values in the attend array */

        printf("Day/Month/Year\n\n");
        for(ap = attend;  ap < attend+12; ap++)
                printf("%d/%d/%d\n", ap -> month, ap -> day, ap ->year);

}
```

One way to pass this structure's data to a function is to pass each int variable individually. We illustrate this by using a function called xmas, which returns TRUE if the date passed is Christmas.

When the variables of the structure today are passed individually, the function call looks like:

```c
xmas(today.month, today.day, today.year)
```

The function xmas is defined as:

```c
xmas(mon,day,year)
      int mon,day,year;
{
        if(mon==12 && day==25)
               return(TRUE);
        return(FALSE);
}
```

A second way to pass the structure's data to a function is to pass the entire structure. Not all C compilers allow structures to be passed to functions, so this feature may not be available with your compiler. However, if this method is available to you, then the structure can be passed as:

```
xmas(today)
```

In this case, the function xmas is defined as:

```
xmas(adate)
    struct date adate; (

    if(adate.month==12 && adate.day==25)
        return(TRUE);
    return(FALSE);


)
```

A third method of passing a structure's data to a function is by passing a pointer to the structure. This feature is implemented by most C compilers that support structures. With this method, you can define a pointer as:

```
struct date *date_pointer;
```

The function call then looks like:

```
date_pointer = &today;
xmas(date_pointer);
```

For this case the function xmas is defined as:

```
xmas(datep)
    struct date *datep; (

    if(datep -> month == 12 && datep -> day == 25)
        return(TRUE);
    return(FALSE);
)
```

FUNCTIONS RETURNING POINTERS TO STRUCTURES

Functions can return pointers to structures just as they can return pointers to int, float, or char. When such a function is defined, you must specify that it will return a pointer to a structure. For example, if func returns a pointer to the date structure defined earlier, its definition begins:

```
struct date *func() {
            .
            .
            .

        }
```

This syntax specifies that func returns a pointer to the structure
type date.

To illustrate such a function, consider the function
match_year. Match_year is a simple function. It will be
defined as:

```
struct date *match_year(dates,size,year)
      struct date *dates;
      int size,year;
```

It is passed the pointer dates, which point to an array of date
structures, an int size, which specifies how many elements are in
the array, and an int year. Match_year scans the array and
returns a pointer to the first element of the array with the
specified year.

Take a look at Listing 7-5. In the for loop, pointer
arithmetic is used to march dateptr from structure to structure.
Because dates is an array of structures, the expression:

```
dateptr < dates + size
```

Listing 7-4. The Matchyear function.

```
      struct date {
             int day;
             int month;
             int year;
      };


      struct date * match_year(dates, size, year)
             struct date *dates;
             int size, year;

      {

             struct date *dateptr;

             for( dateptr = dates ; dateptr < dates + size; dateptr++)
                     if(dateptr -> year == year)
                             return(dateptr);

             return(NULL);

      }
```

verifies that the pointer still points to an array element. The expression:

```
dateptr++
```

increments the pointer by the proper amount so that it points to the next structure in the array.

Program Listing 7-6 tests match_year. It loads an array of structures with arbitrary dates and then calls match_year with some test values. The program output appears as Listing 7-6A.

*THE SIZE OF STRUCTURES

The size of a structure (in bytes) can be determined using the sizeof operator. For example, with the declarations:

```
struct date {
        int month;
        int day;
        int year;
};

int j;
```

The statement:

$$j = sizeof(struct\ date);$$

assigns j a value that is the size of the birth structure in bytes. You cannot assume that the size of a structure is the total size of its elements. If an int is two bytes long a char one byte, and a float four bytes, you cannot assume that:

```
struct {
        int x;
        char c;
        float f;
} example;
```

is seven bytes long. The compiler may need to pad it with a few extra bytes to satisfy various hardware requirements. Rather, determine its size using the expression:

```
sizeof(example)
```

Listing 7-5. Testing matchyear.

```c
#include <stdio.h>
#define NULL  0

struct date {
        int day;
        int month;
        int year;
};

struct date * match_year(dates, size, year)
        struct date *dates;
        int size, year;

{

        struct date *dateptr;

        for( dateptr = dates ; dateptr < dates + size; dateptr++)
                if(dateptr -> year == year)
                        return(dateptr);

        return(NULL);

}


#define DATESIZE  12
struct date dates[DATESIZE];

main()  {

        struct date *ap, *datep;
        int testyear;

        int start_day = 1;
        int start_month = 1;
        int start_year = 1984;

        /* initialize the array dates[] */

        for(ap = dates; ap < dates + DATESIZE; ap++)  {
                ap -> day = start_day++;
                ap -> month = start_month++;
                ap -> year = start_year++;
        }

        /* call match_year with some test years */

        for (testyear = 1980; testyear < 1990; testyear++ )  {
          datep = match_year( dates, DATESIZE, testyear);
          if(datep != NULL)  {
              printf("The year %d matched for the date ", testyear);
              printf("%d /%d /%d \n", datep->month, datep->day, datep->year);

          }
          else
              printf("No match for the year %d \n", testyear);
        }

}
```

Listing 7-5A. Output.

```
No match for the year 1980
No match for the year 1981
No match for the year 1982
No match for the year 1983
The year 1984 matched for the date 1 /1 /1984
The year 1985 matched for the date 2 /2 /1985
The year 1986 matched for the date 3 /3 /1986
The year 1987 matched for the date 4 /4 /1987
The year 1988 matched for the date 5 /5 /1988
The year 1989 matched for the date 6 /6 /1989
```

*SELF-REFERENCING STRUCTURES

You have seen that a structure declaration cannot contain an occurrence of itself. For instance:

```
struct date {
      int month;
      int day;
      int year;
      struct date begin;   /* WRONG */
};
```

is an illegal structure declaration.

Though structures cannot contain occurrences of themselves, they can contain pointers to structures of their own type. For example:

```
struct date {
      int month;
      int day;
      int year;
      struct date *begin;   /* OK */
};
```

is a legal structure declaration. Here the variable begin is a pointer to a date structure, not an embedded occurrence of the date structure.

Structures that contain such pointers are useful for defining certain data structures used in more advanced C programs than those examined here. In Chapter 9 an example of such a program is presented.

Chapter 8

Input, Output, and System Calls

If you scan the list of C keywords shown in Fig. 2-1 you will notice there are no keywords like read, write, input, or print. That is because there are no input/output (I/O) statements in the C language. Rather, functions are supplied by the compiler manufacturer to perform I/O for C programs.

Because I/O is not part of the language, there is variation in the marketplace as to which I/O functions are supplied with a given C compiler. Further, an I/O function may provide capabilities in one compiler that are not provided by an identically-named function in another compiler. Thus, to fully understand the I/O functions of your compiler, you must study your compiler's documentation.

Though standards do not currently exist for C I/O, a great deal of similarity does exist. Many manufacturers have adopted functions from the UNIX standard I/O library. The low level I/O functions (getchar, putchar, getc, putc) are commonly supplied with C compilers. The formatted I/O functions (printf, scanf, fprintf, fscanf) are also commonly supplied. In this chapter we will describe these functions and mention others that may be available to you. We caution that the I/O on your system may differ from the material presented here. By studying your compiler's documentation, experimenting with the I/O functions on your system, and using this material as a guide, you will discover the nature of I/O on your system.

I/O LIBRARY ACCESS

To use the functions supplied in your I/O library, you must include a *header* file in the program. The header file contains definitions and declarations used by the I/O functions.

The name of the header file is dependent upon the compiler you are using. Under UNIX the file is called stdio.h . The preprocessor statement:

```
#include <stdio.h>
```

is used to include the file in the program. If you are using a compiler other than the UNIX C compiler, the header file may have a different name. For example, the preprocessor statement:

```
#include <bdscio.h>
```

is used with the BDS C compiler.

The #include statement is normally written near the beginning of the program. However, you should check your compiler's documentation to determine where the include statement should be placed in the program as well as what file(s) should be included. For instance, the C/80 C compiler recommends that the preprocessor statement:

```
#include "stdlib.c"
```

be used at the end of the program.

As a concluding general rule, you will need to to include a file (or perhaps several files) in your program to use the I/O functions supplied with your compiler.

GETCHAR AND PUTCHAR

Getchar is a function that reads the standard input one character at a time. The standard input is normally the terminal keyboard. In environments that support I/O redirection (such as UNIX) the standard input can be redirected to other devices, files, or programs. This was discussed briefly in Chapter 1.

When using getchar you must remember that getchar returns a value of type int. Hence, when a statement of the form:

```
c = getchar();
```

is used in a program to fetch a value from the standard input, the variable c should be declared as int. If c is declared as char, it will not be able to hold the value returned by getchar to signal end-of-file (EOF). For instance, the following program statements will fail:

```
#include <stdio.h>

main() {
  char c;

  while ( (c = getchar()) !=  EOF)   /* WRONG for char c */
          putchar(c);
```

In this program EOF will never be detected since the value of EOF cannot be stored in a char variable.

Putchar writes one character to the standard output. The standard output is normally the terminal screen. Like the standard input, the standard output can be redirected in environments that support I/O redirection.

The statements:

```
putchar(c);
putchar('a');
putchar('\n');
```

write the contents of the variable c, the letter a, and a new line character on the standard output device. When written to the terminal screen, the C escape sequence \n causes the cursor to move to the beginning of the next line. Table B–1 in Appendix B lists the common C escape sequences.

Though getchar and putchar have been used throughout this text as though they are functions, under UNIX they are implemented as preprocessor macros. Hence, you should not use them in a manner that produces side effects. For example, in Listing 8–1 the argument used with putchar has the side effect of incrementing the pointer. When the preprocessor substitutes replacement text for the statement:

```
putchar(*sp++);
```

Listing 8-1. An example of the incorrect use of putchar.

```
puts(s)  char *s;  {
         /* Write string s to standard output */
         char *sp;

         sp = s;
         while( *sp != '\0' )
                 putchar(*sp++);

}
```

unwanted side effects can occur since the argument *sp++ appears more than once in the replacement text.

PRINTF

Printf is a function that converts its arguments into a format suitable for printing and prints them on the standard output device. From your use of printf in previous chapters, you know that it takes a variable number of arguments, and its form is:

```
printf( format, arg1, arg2, ... )
```

The first argument, format, is a string. The format string can include the following items:

(a) conversion specifications: These specifications begin with a % and end with a conversion character. Examples you have seen are %d, %s, %f, and %c. Conversion specifications will be discussed in detail shortly.

Example: `printf("%d", num);  /* %d conversion spec. */`

(b) C escape sequences: They begin with a \ and are listed in Table B-1. They are printed on the standard output as the character that is represented.

Example: `printf("\t\t");      /*  2 tabs are printed */`

(c) Ordinary characters: They are printed verbatim to the standard output. They are "ordinary" in the sense that they are neither the % character nor an escape sequence.

Example: `printf("Hello world");`

Conversion specifications begin with a % and end with a conversion character. In the conversion specifications:

```
%d   %s   %f   %c
```

the letters d, s, f, and c are conversion characters.

210

Conversion specifications allow you to gain fine control over how a converted argument is printed. For instance, you can control the field width in which the converted argument is printed, whether blanks or zeros should be used to pad field positions not required by the converted argument, and whether the argument should be right or left justified in its print field. When printing float or double data types, you can specify whether the argument should be printed in signed decimal notation or in specific notation, and you can control the number of digits to be printed to the right of the decimal point.

Figure 8-1 is a template to help you learn how to write conversion specifications. It illustrates the position in which information must be placed in a conversion specification. Table 8-1 lists what the template's abbreviations mean.

```
%[ FLAGS ][ FIELD WIDTH ][.][ PRECISION ][ LENGTH MOD ]
[ CONVER CHAR ]
```

Fig. 8-1. Template for writing printf conversions specifications.

The information in Table 8-1 may not apply to the printf function you are using. The tabular data is derived from the printf function supplied with UNIX release 3.0. Check the documentation supplied with your compiler to determine the options available to you for writing conversion specifications. Also, experiment with different conversion specifications to test how printing is formatted.

Given the rules provided in Table 8-1, and the declarations:

```
char buffer[100];
float x;
int i;
```

the following examples are possible conversion specifications:

```
/* Print the first 5 characters of the array buffer */
        printf("%5s", buffer);


/* Using a field of 20 print positions, print the first 15
```

characters from the array buffer left justified in the
field */

```
printf("%-20.15s", buffer);
```

```
/* Using a field of 7 print positions, print x right justified
   (default) with 2 digits printed right of the decimal point */

      printf("%7.2f", x);
```

```
/* Using a field of 6 print positions, print i in decimal notation
   with leading zeros */

      printf("%06d", i);
```

When using printf, remember that the number of conversion specifications in the format argument should agree with the number of arguments to be printed. Also, the type of the argument should be consistent with the type required by the conversion character.

SCANF

Scanf reads characters from the standard input performing conversions directed by conversion specifications. Scanf is the input analog of printf. It is used in the form:

```
scanf(format, ptr_arg1, ptr_arg2, ... )
```

The first argument, format, is a string. Like printf, conversion specifications in the format string direct the conversion of the input characters. The results of the conversions are stored in the memory locations pointed to by the remaining arguments—ptr_arg1, ptr_arg2, etc. These arguments must be pointers.

Conversion specifications begin with a % and end with a conversion character or character class. For example:

```
char d;
scanf("%c", &d);
```

uses the conversion specification %c which directs scanf to read the next character from the standard input. The character read is stored in the variable d. Note that &d is a pointer to d.

When %c is used as a conversion specification, scanf assigns the next input character to the corresponding argument regard-

Table 8-1 Components of printf Conversion Specifications.

[FLAGS]	A minus sign (−). If present, the converted argument is printed left justified in its field. Otherwise, it is printed right justified. A plus sign (+). If present, the corresponding signed conversion will always be preceded by a sign (+ or −). Without this flag, a positive conversion will not be preceded by a + sign. A blank. A negative result of a signed conversion will be preceded with a minus sign while a positive result will be preceded by a blank space. A pound sign (#). The conversion is printed in an alternate form. Octal numbers (the o conversion, see below), are printed with a preceding 0, hexadecimal numbers (the x conversion) are printed with a preceding 0x, floating point numbers (e,E,f,F,g,G conversions) will always contain a decimal point, even when no digits appear after the decimal point. For g and G conversions, trailing zeros will be printed.
[FIELD WIDTH]	An integer which specifies the minimum field width in which the converted argument is printed. If the converted argument requires more print positions than the field width, more will be used. If the converted argument requires fewer print positions than the field width, it is justified according to [FLAGS]. In this case, a pad character is printed in unused field positions. The pad character is normally a blank. However, a zero is used as the pad character if the field width is specified with a leading zero. (Note: this leading zero does not imply that [FIELD WIDTH] is an octal integer).
[.]	A period (.) to separate [FIELD WIDTH] from [PRECISION]
[PRECISION]	An integer. If the argument is a string, it specifies maximum number of characters to be printed from the string. If the argument is float or double, it specifies the maximum number of digits to be printed to the right of the decimal point.
[LENGTH MOD]	The letter l. It specifies that the corresponding argument is long rather than int. It can precede the d,o,u,x, or X conversion characters.
[CONVER CHAR]	The conversion character. It can be one of the following:

d   Convert the argument to signed decimal notation.

u   Convert the argument to unsigned decimal notation.

o   Convert the argument to unsigned octal notation (without a leading 0 See # [FLAGS]).

x   Convert the argument to unsigned hexadecimal notation (without a leading 0x See # [FLAGS]) The letters abcdef are used as hex digits.

X   Like x except the letters ABCDEF are used as hex digits.

c   The argument is a single character.

s   The argument is a string (character pointer). Print characters from the string until a NULL character is reached or until the explicitly specified [PRECISION] is exhausted.

f   The argument is a float or double. Convert it to decimal notation of the form $[\pm]x.yyyyye[\pm]zz$ where the length of the y's is [PRECISION] (default 6). If is 6). If [PRECISION] was explicitly specified as 0, no decimal point is printed.

e   The argument is float or double. Convert it to scientific notation of the form $[+]x.yyyyye[+]zz$ where the length of the y's is [PRECISION] (default 6). If [PRECISION] was explicitly specified as 0, no decimal point is printed.

E   Like e except that an upper case E denotes the exponent field.

g	The argument is float or double. Print it as with an e or f conversion character, using the one which takes up the least space.
G	Like g except the E or f formats are used.
%	Print the % character (i.e. printf("%%");). No argument is involved.

less of what the input character is. For example, if the next input character is a space, a space character is assigned to the corresponding argument.

When conversion characters other than c are used, scanf scans the input looking for the next input field. An input field is a string of contiguous non-white space characters (characters other than space, tab, or newline). For example, the input line:

```
782   319xy   hello 5
```

contains four fields: 782, 391xy, hello, and 5. When scanning for an input field, scanf passes over white space without assigning the white space characters to an argument. Note that scanf will cross line boundaries when scanning for an input field.

The format argument of scanf can contain:

(a) blanks, tabs, or the newline escape sequence (\n) which cause scanf to scan forward to the beginning of the next input field.

(b) conversion specifications which begin with a % and are described below.

(c) an ordinary character which is expected to match the next character read from the input.

Figure 8-2 is a template showing the relative position of components of the scanf conversion specification. Table 8-2 lists the meaning of the components.

The following examples illustrate the use of scanf. In the examples, assume that these declarations have been made:

```
int i,j;
float x,y;
```

```
%[ SKIP ][FIELD WIDTH ][ LENGTH MOD ][ CONVER_CHAR_OR_
CLASS ]
```

Fig. 8-2. Template for writing scanf conversion specifications.

Table 8-2 Components of scanf Conversion Specifications.

[SKIP]	The character *. If present, the next input field is skipped.
[FIELD WIDTH]	An integer. If present, it specifies the maximum width of the input field.
[CONVER__CHAR__OR__CLASS]	The conversion character or a character class. Conversion characters are:

d   A decimal integer is expected.
Corresponding argument should be pointer to int.

o   An octal integer is expected.
Corresponding integer should be pointer to int.

x   A hexadecimal integer is expected.
Corresponding argument should be pointer to int.

D
O
X   A decimal (D), octal (O), or hexadecimal (X) integer is expected as with d,o, and x; but the corresponding argument is a pointer to long.

s   A character string is expected.
Corresponding argument should point to a character array. The array must be large enough to hold the string plus the end-of-string mark \0 which scanf will automatically add. The scan of the input string ends when white space is encountered, or [FIELD WIDTH] is exhausted.

c   A character is expected.
Corresponding argument should be pointer to char. The next character of input is assigned. If the next character is a white space character, it will be assigned.

If [FIELD WIDTH] has been specified (for example, %5c), the argument should point to a char array large enough to hold the characters. No end-of-string mark is added in this case.

e or
f   A floating point number is expected.
Corresponding argument should point to a float. The input characters are optional + or − sign, followed by digits, followed by optional decimal point, followed by optional e or E, followed by optionally signed exponent digits.

The input scan stops when white space or a character incompatible with the above description of input characters is encountered.

E
F   A floating point number is expected as with e or f, but the corresponding argument is pointer to double.

%   The next characer expected is the % sign.

A character class:
A bracket enclosed list of characters (for example, [abcdef]). An input string is read until a character is encountered which is not in the bracketed list. Note that white space does not automatically end the scan.
Example: char digits[80];
           scanf("%[0123456789]", digits);
           Scan stops when a nondigit is encountered.
If the first character inside of the brackets is a circumflex (^), characters are read until an input character matches one of the bracketed characters following the ^.

Example: char nondigits[80];
          scanf("%[^0123456789]",nondigits);

Scan stops when a digit is encountered.

Argument should be pointer to a character array large enough to hold the input string. String is terminated with an end-of-string mark.

[LENGTH—MOD]

The letter l. It may precede the d, o, or x conversion character to indicate that the corresponding argument points to long rather than int. It may precede the e or f conversion characters to indicate that the corresponding argument points to double rather than float.

The letter h. It may precede the d, o, or x conversion character to indicate that the corresponding argument points to short rather than int.

```
double e,f;
char c, s1[80], s2[80];
```

The statement:

```
j = scanf("%c%d%s", &c, &i, s1);
```

with the input line:

```
12345 item1 item2_
```

assigns the character 1 to the variable c, the value 2345 to the variable i, and the string item1 to the array s1. Scanf terminates the string with a /0.

Scanf returns an integer representing the number of arguments successfully assigned. Hence, in the above statement, j is assigned the value three. The next call to scanf (or getchar) will begin scanning (reading) at the blank space following item1.

The statement:

```
scanf("%f%s", &x,s1);
```

will process the input line:

```
-321.57xmy
```

by assigning the value -321.57 to x and the string xmy to the array s1. When scanf is performing a %f conversion, the first character inappropriate for a float number serves to terminate the float input field.

The statement:

```
scanf("%d:%d", &i, &j);
```

will process the input line:

216

```
12:30
```

by assigning 12 to i and 30 to j. The colon in the format argument alerts scanf to expect a colon in the input stream.

Using the declarations:

```
char a,b,c;
char s[2],t[2],r[2];
```

the statement:

```
scanf("%c%c%c", &a,&b,&c);
```

acts on the input line:

```
x y z
```

by assigning x to a, a space character to b, and y to c. The statement:

```
scanf("%1s%1s%1s", s,t,r)
```

acts on the same input line by assigning the strings x, y, and z to the arrays s,t, and r respectively. Note that the conversion specification %c reads the next input character while %1s reads the next non-white space character. Also note that %1s causes scanf to terminate its input with a \0 character.

READING AND WRITING FILES

To this point, all program input has been read from the standard input, and all program output has gone to the standard output. You have seen a method by which the standard input and standard output can be redirected to files. That is one mechanism by which files can be read and written by C programs.

More generally, file I/O can be performed by using a set of functions written specifically for that purpose. Though file I/O functions will vary from compiler to compiler, the principles (and many of the details) are the same.

In general, a file must be opened prior to any access. The function *fopen* performs this task. Once open the file can be accessed using your library's file I/O functions. You need to examine your compiler's documentation to determine which file I/O functions are available to you (several common file I/O functions are described shortly). When your program is finished accessing the file, the function *fclose* is used to close it. Let's look at the details of opening and closing files.

Fopen and Fclose

To open a file, the function fopen is called with two arguments. The form of the function call is:

fopen(filename, access_mode)

Each argument is a string. The first argument, filename, is the name of the file to be opened. The second argument, access_mode, is either of the strings "r", "w", or "a" indicating read, write, or append access respectively. (Three additional access modes for updating files are available with UNIX Release 3. They are not described here.)

Fopen determines whether the file actually exists and, in UNIX environments, whether you have permission to access it. If you are attempting to write or append to a nonexistent file, fopen will try to create the file for you. Fopen returns a value which you can store in a program variable. The value serves to identify the file. It is used to subsequently read from or write to the file. If a value of 0 (null) is returned, the file could not be opened due to some error condition.

A file can be opened in one of three access modes—read, write, or append. In the following examples of fopen, data.inp, data.out, and data.log represent file names, while infile, outfile, and logfile are program variable names. The program variables must be declared prior to use. How they are declared will vary depending on the compiler you are using. We will address the declarations shortly. Within the description of access modes you can ignore mention of file access permission if you are using CP/M or MS-DOS.

- Read Access Mode:

  Example: `infile = fopen("data.inp", "r");`

  If a file named data.inp exists (and you have permission to read it) a non-zero value is returned by fopen; otherwise, zero (null) is returned.
- Write Access Mode:

  Example: `outfile = fopen("data.out","w");`

  If a file named data.out exists (and you have permission to write it) the file's contents are erased and a non-zero value is returned by fopen. If the file does not exist, fopen tries to create it. A non-zero value is returned if data.out is successfully created. Otherwise, zero (null) is returned.

A successful open in write mode thus guarantees an initially empty file.

● Append Mode:

Example: `logfile = fopen("data.log","a");`

If a file named data.log exists (and you have write permission), the file is opened and its contents are preserved. A non-zero value is returned by fopen. Any output your program performs to this file is appended to the end of the file.

If the file does not exist, fopen trys to create it. The value returned is nonzero if the file was successfully created, otherwise zero (null) is returned.

The way in which the program variables infile, outfile, and logfile are declared and the type of value returned by fopen are the principal differences between UNIX C programs and C programs written for many of the CP/M and MS-DOS compilers.

Under UNIX, the type name FILE is defined in stdio.h, and fopen returns a pointer to a FILE type. Thus, for our examples, the UNIX C declarations and calls to fopen would appear as follows:

```
/* Opening files under UNIX  */
#include <stdio.h>
FILE *infile, *outfile, *logfile;
FILE *fopen();

main() {
        infile = fopen("data.inp", "r");
        outfile = fopen("data.out", "w");
        logfile = fopen("data.log", "a");
               .
               .
               .
```

Note that FILE is in all capital letters and that fopen must be declared prior to use. The value returned by fopen is called a *file pointer.*

Though some CP/M and MS-DOS C compilers follow the UNIX convention, many do not. When the UNIX convention is not followed, fopen usually returns an int. Hence, the declarations and calls to fopen appear as:

```
/* Opening files with many CP/M and MS-DOS compilers */

#include <stdio.h>

int infile, outfile, logfile;

main() {

        infile = fopen("data.inp", "r");
        outfile = fopen("data.out", "w");
        logfile = fopen("data.log","a");
                        .
                        .
                        .


}
```

Note that in this case fopen need not be declared because int is the default return type for functions. The variables used to hold the values returned by fopen are declared as type int. Of course you can add the statement:

```
#define FILE int
```

early in the program and declare these variables as:

```
FILE infile, outfile, logfile;
```

This #define aids in documenting your program by identifying these int variables as references to files. These variables are generally called file descriptors.

The arguments to fopen need not be string literals. They can be pointers to strings as in:

```
char input[] = "datafile";

infile = fopen(input, "r");
```

Further, it is common practice to embed the call to the fopen function in an if statement. This usage appears as follows:

```
if( (infile = fopen(input, "r")) == NULL)
     printf("couldn't open %s\n", input);
else
        /* the file opened successfully*/
```

You have seen how to open a file using UNIX C compilers and non-UNIX C compilers that use integer file descriptors. When the program is finished accessing the file, the function

220

fclose is used to close it. The argument to fclose is the value that was returned by fopen. For example, if the file was opened as:

```
infile = fopen("data.dat", "r");
```

it would be closed with the statement:

```
fclose(infile);
```

Fclose returns a value of 0 (null) if the file was successfully closed. A non-zero value indicates that some error ocurred while closing the file. The value returned by fclose can be tested in the usual manner:

```
if( fclose(infile) != NULL )
    printf("Error closing file\n");
```

With the methods for opening and closing files behind you, you can move on to reading information from files and writing information to them.

Getc and Putc

Once open, the file can be read character by character using getc, or written a character at a time using putc. Getc is used as:

```
getc( file_ref )
```

where file_ref is a value returned by fopen. Getc is like getchar except that getc reads from the file indentified by file_ref while getchar reads from the standard input. As with getchar, getc returns an int so the value EOF (-1) can be returned to indicate end-of-file. Program Listings 8-2 and 8-3 illustrate the use of getc to read a file. The program prompts the user for a file name, then attempts to open the named file for reading. If the file opens successfully, the program displays it on the terminal. I/O to the terminal is handled by scanf, putchar, and printf. Getc is used to read the file.

Two versions of the program are shown (Listing 8-2 and Listing 8-3). The first version, written for UNIX C or compatible compilers, uses FILE pointers. The second version is written for compilers that use integer file descriptors.

Putc is used as:

```
putc(c,file_ref)
```

where c is the character to be written, and file_ref is a value

221

returned by fopen. Putc is analogous to putchar except that putc
writes to the file identified by file_ref rather than to the standard
output.

Program Listing 8-4 illustrates the use of getc and putc in a
file copying application. Assume that the executable version of
the program is called "copyfile." If copyfile is invoked as:

```
copyfile in_name out_name
```

the program writes a copy of the file in_name to the file
out_name. Clearly, the program must read its command line
arguments. The command line arguments were initially discussed in Chapter 6.

Two versions of the program (Listings 8-4 and 8-5) are
shown. The first version uses UNIX FILE pointers. It also uses
the exit system call. When the exit call is encountered in a
program, the program terminates and control passes to the
operating system. Syntactically, the exit call looks like a
function call with one argument. In UNIX environments, the
argument is used to indicate whether the program terminated
sucessfully or with an error. An argument of zero in the exit call
conventionally indicates success. A nonzero argument indicates an error exit condition. An exit call is available with
most C compilers.

Listing 8-2. Using getc to read a file, (UNIX style I/O.)

```
        /* Version 1 */

        #define NULL 0
        #include <stdio.h>

        main()  {  /*  Display a file on the terminal screen.  Uses UNIX
                        style file pointers.  */

                char filename[50];
                FILE *infile, *fopen();
                int i,c;

                printf("Enter name of file to display>");
                scanf("%s", filename);

                if( (infile = fopen(filename, "r") ) == NULL )
                        printf("Couldn't open %s\n", filename);
                else {
                        /* Read characters from the file */
                        while( (c = getc(infile)) != EOF )
                                putchar(c);  /* write to screen */

                        fclose(infile);      /* close file */
                }

        }
```

Listing 8-3. Using getc to read a file (non UNIX style I/O)

```
/* Version 2 */

#define NULL 0
#include <stdio.h>

#define FILE int

main()  {    /* Display a file on the terminal screen.  Uses integer file
                descriptors common with microcomputer C compilers */

        char filename[50];
        FILE infile;
        int i,c;

        printf("Enter name of file to display>");
        scanf("%s", filename);

        if( (infile = fopen(filename, "r") ) == NULL )
                printf("Couldn't open %s\n", filename);
        else  {
                /* Read characters from the file */
                while( (c = getc(infile)) != EOF )
                        putchar(c);  /* write to screen */

                fclose(infile);      /* close file */
        }

}
```

Program listing 8-5 uses integer file descriptors. It does not use the exit call. Though getc and putc perform I/O "character by character," the actual disk access is not performed on a character by character basis. Rather, when getc is used, large disk blocks are read by other system functions and returned to your program one character at a time. Similarly, characters written by putc are stored by other system functions and written to the disk in a larger chunk than a single character. Thus, you need not be concerned that these functions are inefficient for disk access.

Fprintf and Fscanf

The functions fprintf and fscanf perform formatted I/O on open files in the manner that printf and scanf perform formatted I/O on the standard output and standard input, respectively. The syntax of fprintf is:

```
fprintf(outfile, format, arg1, arg2,...)
```

where outfile is a value returned by fopen. The format argument is just like the format argument used with printf.

223

Listing 8-4. Copy a file (UNIX Style I/O).

```
/* copyfile version 1.   Uses UNIX FILE pointers and the exit system call. */

#define NULL 0
#include   <stdio.h>

main(argc, argv)
        int argc;
        char *argv[];   (    /* Copy file named in argv[1] to file name in
                                argv[2] */

        FILE *infile, *outfile, *fopen();
        int c;

        if(argc != 3)   (
                printf("Usage: copyfile infile outfile\n");
                exit(1);
        )

        if( (infile = fopen(argv[1], "r") ) == NULL)  (
                printf("Couldn't open input file %s\n", argv[1]);
                exit(2);
        )

        if( (outfile = fopen(argv[2], "w") ) == NULL)  (
                printf("Couldn't open output file %s\n", argv[2]);
                exit(3);
        )

        /*  Read infile, write outfile */
        while( (c = getc(infile) ) != EOF)
                putc(c, outfile);

        /* close files, normal exit */
        fclose(infile); fclose(outfile);
        exit(0);
)
```

Program Listing 8-6 uses fprintf to write lines of text into a file. Assume that the executable version of the program is in a file named filetext. If it's invoked as:

```
filetext datafile
```

the program writes text typed at the terminal to the file named datafile. On the other hand, if it is invoked as:

```
filetext datafile -a
```

the program appends the text to the file named datafile. The program reads lines of text with getline until a line with only a carriage return is typed. It uses integer file descriptors. If your system uses UNIX style file pointers, modify this program as shown in the last section.

224

The syntax of fscanf is:

```
fscanf(infile, format, ptr_agr1, ptr_arg2,...)
```

where infile is a value returned by fopen. Fscanf converts its arguments according to the conversion specification in the format argument.

Fscanf reads characters from the file identified by infile and performs the conversions specified by the format argument. The format argument contains conversion specifications written

Listing 8-5. Copy a file (non UNIX style I/O).

```
/*  Copyfile version 2.  Uses integer file descriptors.  Does not
    use the exit call */

#define NULL 0
#include <stdio.h>

#define FILE int

main(argc, argv)
      int argc;
      char *argv[];  {   /*  Copy file named in argv[1] to file named
                              in argv[2] */

      FILE infile, outfile;
      int c;

      if(argc == 3)
            if( (infile = fopen(argv[1], "r") ) != NULL)
                  if( (outfile = fopen(argv[2], "w") ) != NULL)  {
                                    /* both files opened ok, copy */
                        while( (c = getc(infile) ) != EOF)
                                    putc(c, outfile);
                        fclose(infile); fclose(outfile);
                  }else
                        printf("Couldn't open output file %s\n", argv[2]);
            else
                        printf("Couldn't open input file %s\n", argv[1]);
      else
            printf("Usage: copyfile infile outfile\n");

}
```

Listing 8-6. A sample of program using Fprintf.

```
         #include <stdio.h>
         #define TRUE  1
         #define FALSE  0

         #define FILE int

         #include "getline.c"
         #define MAXTEXT  100

main(argc,argv)
         int argc;
         char *argv[];
(
         char *access_mode;
         char *write = "w";
         char *append = "a";

         FILE outfile;

         char text[MAXTEXT];

         if(argc == 3  && argv[2][0] == '-'  && argv[2][1] == 'a')
                 access_mode = append;
         else  if(argc == 2)
                 access_mode = write;
         else  (
                 printf("Usage: filetext filename [-a]\n");
                 exit(1);
         )

         if( (outfile = fopen(argv[1], access_mode) ) == NULL)  (
                 printf("Couldn't open %s\n", argv[1]);
                 exit(2);
         )

         printf("Enter text for the file %s\n", argv[1]);
                 if( getline(text, MAXTEXT) <= 1)
             else
                     fprintf(outfile, "%s", text);
         )
      fclose(outfile);

   )
```

like those for scanf. As with scanf, the arguments ptr_arg1,
ptr_arg2, etc. must be pointers.

STDIN, STDOUT, STDERR

Recall that a successful call to fopen of the form:

```
file_ref = fopen("datafile", "r");
```

sets file_ref to a value used in function calls to read datafile.
Three such values are automatically defined for you. They are

stdin, stdout, and stderr. They can be used to read the standard input, or write to the standard output, or standard error file.

For instance, each of the function calls:

```
c = getchar();
c = getc(stdin);
```

read a character from the standard input. The calls:

```
putchar(c);
putc(c, stdout);
```

each write a character to the standard output.

The standard error file has not been discussed previously. It is used for output, and like the standard output file it is normally the terminal screen. The standard error file is a useful place to write error messages. Consider the statements:

```
printf("Hello");
fprintf(stderr,"Error occurred");
```

If output has not been redirected, both statements will print information on the terminal. However, if the standard output has been redirected to a file, only the second message (Error occurred) is printed on the terminal. In this way, stderr can be used to keep error messages from going into files when I/O has been redirected.

CREAT, UNLINK

In your program you can explicitly request that a file be created by using the system call creat (note, there is no final e on creat). Using UNIX C compilers, creat returns a file pointer. Thus, prior to use, the creat function is declared as:

FILE *creat( );

For compilers using integer file descriptors, creat returns an int.
Creat is used as:

```
creat(filename)
```

where the string filename serves to name the file. Under UNIX, if the attempt to create the file fails, creat returns 0 (null); when successful, a non-zero value is returned. If your compiler uses integer file descriptors, check your documentation to determine the values returned by creat to signal success and failure.

Example:

```
if(creat("tempfile.$$") == 0) {
```

```
printf("Couldn't create tempfile.$$");
exit(1);
}
```

Unlink is used to delete a file. It is called as:

```
unlink(filename)
```

If successful, the file named by the string filename is deleted from the file system (e.g., the disk) and a non-zero value is returned. If the call is not successful, a value of 0 (null) is returned.

Example:

```
unlink("tempfile.$$");
```

SPRINTF, SSCANF

Sprintf performs conversions like printf, but it writes its output into a character array in memory. It is used as:

```
sprintf(memory_buffer, format, arg1, arg2,...)
```

where memory_buffer is the name of a character array sufficiently long to hold the output.

Sscanf reads characters from an internal memory area performing conversions. It is used as:

```
sscanf(read_buffer, format, ptr_arg1, ptr_arg2...)
```

The characters read from read_buffer are converted according to format and the results are stored at the memory locations pointed to by ptr_arg1, ptr_arg2, and so on.

Chapter 9

Advanced Topics

In this chapter several features of C will be discussed. First, the typedef statement is introduced. The typedef statement lets you create new names for existing C data types. Not all C compilers implement the typedef statement, so this statement may not be available on your system.

Next recursion is discussed. An object is called recursive if it is defined in terms of itself. As we discuss recursion you will examine some examples of recursive C functions—functions which call themselves.

Pointers to functions is the next topic. You will see that the address of a function can be stored in a pointer variable and that this address can be passed to other functions.

Following this discussion bit level operations are introduced. The ability to conveniently manipulate data at the bit level is a feature of C that has helped to make it an attractive systems programming language. Our discussion introduces the bitwise operators and bit fields.

The concluding sections of the chapter address unions,

additional preprocessor statements, and language issues regarding programs that span several files.

TYPEDEF

The typedef statement is used to create synonyms for other data types. For example, the statement:

```
typedef char BYTE;
```

defines the name **BYTE** to be a synonym for char. Subsequently, declarations of the form:

```
BYTE c,p,s[10];
```

can be used. The statement:

```
typedef float REAL, DOLLARS;
```

creates two synonyms for float. The synonyms are written in all capital letters for emphasis.

One use of typedef is to enhance the documentation of a program. For instance, with the typedef statement:

```
typedef int LOGICAL;
```

a function definition beginning:

```
LOGICAL funca() { ...
```

can alert a reader of the program that funca returns a value which is interpreted as true or false.

A second use of typedef is to aid in the portability of a program. For example, a data type name SMALLINT could be created. On one machine it might be appropriate to use:

```
typedef short SMALLINT
```

while on another machine, perhaps:

```
typedef int SMALLINT
```

is a better choice. In either event, if the type name SMALLINT is spread throughout the program, all SMALLINT declarations are affected by changing the typedef statement and recompiling the program.

A third use of typedef is to create a simple name for a complex declaration. For example:

```
typedef struct node {

    char name[NAMESIZE];
    int count;
    struct node *forward;
    struct node *backward;

} LISTNODE;
```

creates the type name **LISTNODE** as a synonym for the structure declaration. Following this typedef, declarations of the node structure can appear as:

```
LISTNODE x,y,*z;
```

This declaration defines two of the node structures (x and y) and one pointer to a node structure (z).

As an aid in remembering how to write a typedef statement, compare it to a variable storage class and type declaration. For example:

```
static int count;   /* variable declaration*/

typedef int COUNTER;   /*the typedef*/
```

Note that "typedef" occupies the same relative position as the storage class specifier (static), and the new type name (**COUNTER**) is in the position of the variable (count).

Some of the features provided by typedef can be accomplished using #define. For instance:

```
typedef char BYTE;

#define BYTE char
```

have the same affect on a program. However, typedef can cope with C program syntax which exceeds the capabilities of the preprocessor. For example:

```
typedef char *STRING;
```

makes **STRING** a synonym for char *****. Subsequently, declarations like

```
STRING s,t;
```

declare s and t as pointers to char. The statement:

```
typedef char *STRING_FUNC();
```

makes **STRING_FUNC** a synonym for "function returning a pointer to char." Subsequently, you can make declarations like:

```
STRING_FUNC func;
```

to mean:

```
char *func();
```

Similarly, the statement:

```
typedef char PRINT_LINE[132];
```

makes **PRINT_LINE** a synonym for "char array of size 132." A statement can now be written as:

```
PRINT_LINE heading, footer;
```

which is the same as writing:

```
char heading[132], footer[132];
```

In the next section, there is an example program where the typedef statement is used.

RECURSION

C functions may call themselves either directly or indirectly. Such use is called recursion. A simple example is a recursive implementation of the factorial function.

In mathematics, *n factorial* is denoted n!, and defined to be n x (n-1) x ... x 1. For example, 5! is 5 x 4 x 3 x 2 x 1 or 120. 0! is defined to be 1. The factorial function can be written recursively as:

```
factorial(n) int n; {
        /* n! for nonnegative n */
            int j;

            j = n;
            if(j==0)
                    return (1);
            return(j * factorial(j-1));

}
```

232

Figure 9-1 illustrates the effect of the program:

```
main() {
        int k;
        k = factorial(3);
        printf("%d", k);

}
```

In this example, the factorial function is invoked four times. Each invocation of the factorial function gets a private and distinct set of automatic variables (j in this case).

The factorial function can be written quite simply as a nonrecursive function:

```
factorial(n) int n; {
        /* n! for nonnegative n*/

        int fact;
        if(n==0)
                return(1);
        for(fact =1; n > 0; n--)
                fact *= n;

        return(fact);

}
```

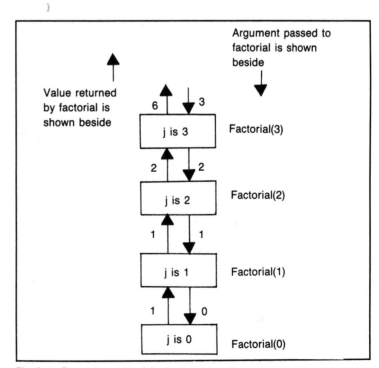

Fig. 9-1. Recursive calls of the factorial function.

Listing 9-1. Recursion example.

```
/* putit.c */

#include <stdio.h>

int num = 0;

main() {
        putit();
}

putit() {
        printf("hello\n");
        if (++num < 10 )
                putit();
}
```

As another example of recursion, guess what is printed by Listing 9-1. Try running the program on your system.

Recursion is quite useful with data structures defined recursively. A tree is such a data structure. A *tree* is a hierarchical data structure composed of nodes. A *node* is like a compartment where information is stored. One node is distinguished from the others and is called the *root*. Figure 9-2 shows a picture of a tree. This tree represents the hierarchy of a book. The root node is labeled **BOOK**.

Though a formal definition of a tree is beyond the scope of this book, intuitively you can see that a tree is a branching

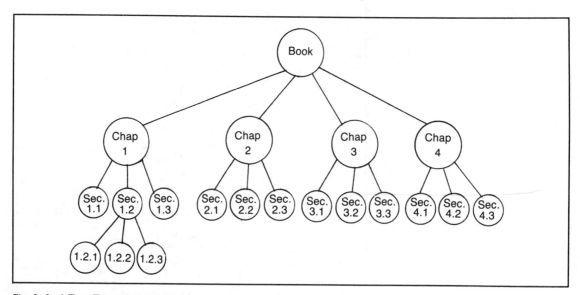

Fig. 9-2. A Tree Example.

structure emanating from a root node. Observe that if the portion of the tree emanating from the CHAP1 node is displayed by itself (Fig. 9-3) it, too, is a tree (called a subtree of the original tree). This suggests that a tree can be defined recursively.

A tree is empty (or null) if it doesn't have any nodes. A special type of tree—a binary tree— is one in which each node has two subtrees. They are called the left subtree and the right subtree. One or both of the subtrees may be null.

To illustrate how recursion can be used in C, Listing 9-2 stores data (integers) in a binary tree. The first integer read is stored in the root node. Subsequent integers are stored by marching down the tree going left if the new integer is smaller than the value currently at a node, or right if it is larger. For example, Fig. 9-4 shows the resulting binary tree if the integers 12, 3, 21, 17, 2, and 5 are read.

If for each node you print the integers in its left subtree, followed by the integer at the node, then the integers in the right subtree, the integers will be printed as:

```
2,3,5,12,17,21
```

The integers are printed in increasing order (see Exercise 1). The program in Listing 9-2 reads integers, stores them in a binary tree, and prints them in increasing order. You can print the contents of the tree at any time by entering the integer 1, or stop the program by entering the integer 0. The program uses recursion as well as the typedef statement discussed in the last section.

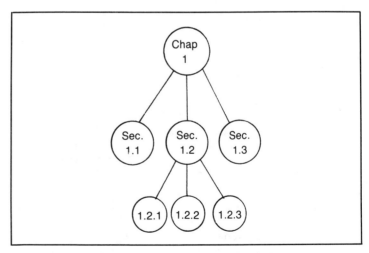

Fig. 9-3. A Subtree of The Tree Illustrated in Fig. 9-2.

235

Listing 9-2. An example of recursion using a binary tree.

```
#define NULL 0
#include <stdio.h>

typedef struct node {
        int num;
        struct node *left;
        struct node *right;
} TREENODE;

char *calloc();


TREENODE * getnode() {   /* get memory for a TREENODE */
        return ( (TREENODE *)calloc(1, sizeof(TREENODE) )  );
}

TREENODE * putin_tree(num, treeptr)
        int num;
        TREENODE * treeptr;

{       /* store num in the tree rooted at treeptr */

        if( treeptr == NULL)  /* get a new node to store num */
                if( (treeptr = getnode() ) == NULL )
                        return(NULL);  /* out of space */
                else {
                        treeptr->num = num;
                        treeptr->left = treeptr->right = NULL;
                        return(treeptr);
                }

        /* treeptr points to a node in the tree.  Store num in the
           appropriate subtree  */

        if( num > treeptr->num)  /* store num in right subtree */
                treeptr->right = putin_tree(num, treeptr->right);
        else if( num < treeptr->num)  /* store num in left subtree */
                treeptr->left = putin_tree(num, treeptr->left);
        return(treeptr);
}


print_tree( treeptr )
        TREENODE * treeptr; {

        /* Print integers in left subtree, then the node , then
           right subtree  */

        if(treeptr != NULL) {
                print_tree(treeptr->left);
                printf("%d\n", treeptr->num);
                print_tree(treeptr->right);
        }
}


main() {
        TREENODE * root = NULL;
        int value;
```

```
        printf("\n\t\tENTER INTEGERS.\n\n");
        printf("\t\t\t0 will stop the program\n");
        printf("\t\t\t1 will print the tree\n\n");
        printf("\t\tALL OTHER VALUES WILL BE STORED\n");

while(1) {
        printf("\nEnter Integer>");
        scanf("%d", &value);
        if (value == 0)
                break;
        if(value == 1)
                print_tree(root);
        else
                root = putin_tree(value,root);
        }
    }
```

POINTERS TO FUNCTIONS

In C you can declare a variable to be a pointer to a function. This pointer can be used to execute the function to which it points. Pointers to functions may be a useful feature of your C compiler. For instance, many C compilers are delivered with prewritten sorting functions. These functions will out-perform the bubblesort function discussed in Chapter 5. To use the prewritten sorting functions, you must pass them pointers to other functions.

As an example, the prewritten function qsort begins as:

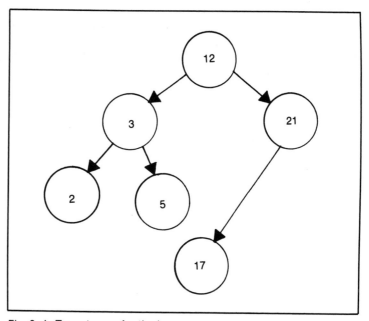

Fig. 9-4. Tree storage for the input sequence 12, 3, 21, 17, 2, 5.

```
qsort(data, num_of_elements, element_width, compare)
       char *data;
       int num_of_elements;
       int element_width;
       int (*compare)();     /* NEW */
```

The declaration:

```
int (*compare)();
```

is new. It declares the variable compare to be a pointer to a function that returns an int. The first set of parentheses is required as:

```
int *compare();
```

means "function returning pointer to int."

To use qsort, you must pass it:

- data: a pointer to the beginning of the data elements to be sorted.
- num_of_elements: the number of data elements.
- element_width: the width of each data element in bytes.
- compare: a pointer to a function which compares two data elements. The function is passed pointers to two data elements. The function returns: 0 if data element-1 == data element-2; a negative value if data element-1 < data element-2; a positive value if data element-1 > data element-2.

Now suppose that the two dimensional array:

```
char name[MAXNAMES][NAMESIZE];
```

is to be sorted. Then a suitable compare function is strcmp:

```
strcmp(s,t) char *s, *t;
{
       while(*s++ == *t++)
             if(*s == '\0')
                        return(0);
       return(*s - *t);
}
```

238

Now qsort can be called to sort the array:

```
qsort(name, MAXNAMES, NAMESIZE, strcmp);
```

Note that the name strcmp is passed as the last argument. The name of a function is a pointer to the function just as an array name is a pointer to the array.

BIT LEVEL OPERATIONS

At the lowest level all data within the computer is stored as zeros and ones. As is discussed in Appendix A, the zeros and ones are called bits. C allows you to manipulate data at the bit level; the C bitwise operators are used for this purpose. In this section we discuss bit level manipulation of data. If you are not familiar with the bit level view of data, refer to Appendix A before reading this section.

AND, OR, XOR, and COMPLEMENT Operators. For two binary digits (bits), the AND operation follows the rules:

```
0 AND 0 = 0
0 AND 1 = 0
1 AND 0 = 0
1 AND 1 = 1
```

the value of the AND operation is one only when both its operands are one. Using this definition, when the AND operator is applied to two eight-bit operands, then:

```
      10101101
AND   11101000
      --------
      10101000
```

The 0 and 1 in these examples represent single bits rather than integers.

The OR operation results in a value of one when either of its operands (or both) have the value one. Thus:

```
0 OR 0 = 0
0 OR 1 = 1
1 OR 0 = 1
1 OR 1 = 1
```

Consequently, when eight-bits operands are considered, the OR operation appears as:

```
01010101
```

```
OR   11000110
    ----------
     11010111
```

The XOR (eXclusive OR) operation is similar to the OR. It results in the value one when either of its operands (but not both) are one. Hence, for single bit operands, the XOR operation follows the rules:

```
0 XOR 0 = 0
0 XOR 1 = 1
1 XOR 0 = 1
1 XOR 1 = 0
```

When applied to eight bits, the operation is exemplified by:

```
      10101110
XOR   10010100
      ----------
      00111010
```

The COMPLEMENT operator is a unary operator. It flips the bits of its operand. So, the COMPLEMENT of zero is one and the COMPLEMENT of one is zero. The COMPLEMENT of 00110011 is 11001100.

These bit level operations can be performed in C by using the appropriate C operator. In C, the operators are written using the symbols shown below:

Bit Level Operation	C Operator
AND	&
OR	|
XOR	^
COMPLÉMENT	~

The bitwise operators can be applied to variables that are declared as char or int (including unsigned, long, and short). C statements using these operators look like:

```
z = x & y;      /* AND operator */
z = x | y;      /* OR operator */
z = x ^ y;      /* XOR operator */
z = ~x;         /* COMPLEMENT operator */
```

Bit Packing. One use of the bit level operators is to pack information into a single variable that might otherwise use more memory. To do this, note that when a number is a power of two, it has a binary representation with exactly one one-bit.

240

For instance, Table 9-1 shows the decimal, octal, and binary representations of the first eight powers of 2 (2^0, 2^1, ..., 2^7). When a bit has the value one, it is said to be *on* or *set*. When it has the value *zero,* it is called *off,* or *clear.* Observe that the binary representation of each number in the table has exactly one bit that is on.

Now consider a mailing list application where you wish to assign various attributes to entries in the list. For example, consider attributes that specify whether the given entry is a friend, business associate, or family member; or whether the addressee should be mailed a Christmas card. Further, an entry should be able to have several attributes simultaneously. For instance, a business associate may also be on the Christmas card list. Using bit level operations, the mailing list attributes can be maintained in a single variable. For example, with the #define statements:

```
#define XMAS 01
#define BUSINESS 02
#define FRIEND 04
#define FAMILY 010
```

and the int variable mail_type, the following program statements illustrate the approach:

```
mail_type = 0;              /* turn all of mail_type's bits off */

mail_type = mail_type | XMAS;          /* turn the XMAS bit on */

mail_type = mail_type | BUSINESS | FRIEND; /* turn both BUSINESS
                                     and FRIEND bits on */

mail_type = mail_type & ~FREIND;    /* turn the FRIEND bit off */

mail_type = mail_type & ~(XMAS | BUSINESS);    /* turn XMAS and
                                  BUSINESS off */
```

Table 9-1. The Decimal, Octal, and Binary Number Systems.

Decimal	Octal	Binary
1	01	000000001
2	02	000000010
4	04	000000100
8	010	000001000
16	020	000010000
32	040	000100000
64	0100	001000000
128	0200	010000000

Using the bitwise operators, you can consider an attribute present if the appropriate bit is on, or absent if the bit is off.

These operators can be used in the operational assignment form (Chapter 4), so the above statements can be written:

```
mail_type |= XMAS;
mail_type |= BUSINESS | FRIEND;
mail_type &= ~FRIEND;
mail_type &= ~(XMAS | FRIEND);
```

Note the OR operator is used to turn bits on, while bits are turned off using AND and COMPLEMENT. In the statement:

```
mail_type &= ~(XMAS | FRIEND)
```

the parentheses are necessary because the COMPLEMENT operator has a higher precedence than the OR operator. Table 9-2 shows the precedence of these and all other C operators.

You can test whether the bits are on or off in a program with statements like:

```
if(mail_type & FRIEND) {
    /* the FRIEND bit is on */
            .
            .
            .

}

else {
    /*FRIEND bit is off */

}
```

Be careful to distinguish the bitwise operators & and || from the logical connective && and || ||. For instance, in:

```
if(mail_type & FRIEND || mail_type & XMAS) {
    /* true if either FRIEND or XMAS bit is on */
            .
            .
            .

}
```

both the bitwise AND operator and the logical connective || are used.

Shift Operators. The shift operators perform left and right shifts of their operands by a specified number of bits. For

Table 9-2. Precedence of All C Operators.

Operator Use	Operator Symbol	Associativity
function calls array references struct member struct member via pointer	() [] . ->	Left To Right
COMPLEMENT address-of indirection unary minus increment, decrement cast, sizeof negation	~ & * — ++ —— (type) sizeof !	Right To Left
multiply, divide modulus	* / %	Left To Right
add, subtract	+	Left To Right
bitwise left shift bitwise right shift	<< >>	Left To Right
relational	< <= > >=	Left To Right
equality, inequality	== !=	Left To Right
bitwise AND	&	Left To Right
bitwise XOR	^	Left To Right
bitwise OR	|	Left To Right
logical connective and	&&	Left To Right
logical connective or	||	Left To Right
conditional	?:	Right To Left
assignment	= += -= *= /= %= &= ^= |= >>= <<=	Right To Left
sequential execution	,	Left To Right

Note: Operators between horizontal bars have same precedence and associativity. Top of table is the highest precedence operators.

example, if n has the value eight, its bit pattern is 00001000. The statement:

```
n >> 3;
```

shifts the bits in n three places to the right, which results in the bit pattern 00000001. Again when n has the value eight, the statement:

```
n << 2
```

shifts the bits two to the left, resulting in the bit pattern 00100000.

When n has the value two, its bit pattern is 0010. The statement:

```
n = n << 1;
```

changes the bit pattern to 0100, which is four. So, a left shift by one bit performs a multiplication by two; a left shift by two bits is a multiplication by four, a left shift by k bits is a multiplication by 2^k. Similarly, right shifts perform division.

When bits are shifted to the left, zero bits are filled in on the right. The right shift operator will fill vacated bits with zero on the left if the operand has been declared unsigned. Right-shifting a signed quantity (such as an int) may fill the vacated bit with a zero or a one depending upon the machine and compiler you are using.

Shift operators can be used in the operational assignment form, as in:

```
n >>= 4;
```

which is equivalent to:

```
n = n >> 4;
```

Bit Fields. Previously you saw the bitwise operators used to maintain the mail list attributes **XMAS, BUSINESS, FRIEND,** and **FAMILY.** These attributes can also be maintained using fields.

A field is a set of adjacent bits within a single int. To define fields, a syntax similar to structure definition is used. For example:

```
struct {

      unsigned xmas : 1;
      unsigned business : 1;
      unsigned friend : 1;
      unsigned family : 1;

} mail_type;
```

defines a variable called mail_type which contains four one-bit fields. The individual fields are named xmas, business, friend, and family. The :1 following each name specifies that the field is one bit wide. These fields behave like small unsigned numbers. Hence they are declared unsigned.

244

Individual fields are accessed like structure members are accessed. For instance, they can be assigned values with statements like:

```
mail_type.xmas = 1;
mail_type.business = 1;
mail_type.friend = 0;
```

They can be tested as:

```
if(mail_type.xmas ==1)...
```

or

```
if(mail_type.xmas == 1 && mail_type.family == 0)...
```

Because the fields in this example are one bit wide, only the values zero and one can be assigned to them. If a field is defined as two bits wide, the values 0,1,2, and 3 can be assigned to them. Similarly, a field three bits wide can accept values in the range 0-7; etc.

Bit fields can be assigned values, tested, and used in arithmetic expressions. They do not have addresses, so the address-of operator can not be applied to them.

UNIONS

The *union* is a C language construct which lets different types of data items share the same location in memory. The syntax to define and access a union is like that for structures. For example, the statement:

```
union {

    char alpha;
    int num;
} mem;
```

defines a variable called mem which can hold either a char or an int. When mem is accessed as a character variable, it is accessed as:

```
mem.alpha
```

When it is accessed as an int variable, it is accessed as:

```
mem.num
```

When you use unions you must keep track of the type of information currently stored in the union. For example, with the declarations:

```
#define CHARACTER    1
#define INTEGER      2

union  {
     char alpha;
     int num;
}  mem;

int utype;
```

The statements:

```
mem.alpha = 'a';
utype = CHARACTER;
```

place a character into the union. The variable utype is used to indicate the type of data the union currently holds. To print the union, the following statements could be used:

```
if(utype == CHARACTER)
     printf("%c", mem.alpha);
else if(utype == INTEGER)
     printf("%d", mem.num);
```

MULTI-FILE C PROGRAMS

The source code that comprises one C program can be spread over several files. Even when this is done, functions defined in one source file can access global variables defined in another file. To accomplish this, the keyword *extern* is used. For example, suppose filea.c contains the source code:

```
int count;

bumpcount()  {
     count++;

}
```

and fileb.c contains the source code:

```
main()  {

     int i;
     extern int count;
```

```
        count = 100;
        for(i = 0; i < 10; i++)
                bumpcount();
        printf("%d",count);

}
```

In filea.c, the declaration:

```
int count;
```

"defines" the variable—it causes memory to be allocated for count. The declaration:

```
extern int count;
```

in fileb.c does not cause memory to be allocated. Rather, it states that the variable count is defined elsewhere.

When these two files are compiled and the resulting object modules linked together, the count variable in each file will refer to the same memory location. When executed, the program prints: 110.

The commands required to compile and link the files depends on the system you are using. With UNIX, the command:

```
cc filea.c fileb.c
```

will suffice. The cc command will invoke the compiler, then the linker, and produce an executable file named a.out. Other C compilers may require a two-step process such as:

```
cc filea.c fileb.c
link filea fileb
```

Note that in fileb.c the function bumpcount was not declared as an external function. When a function is not declared the compiler assumes that it returns int. If bumpcount returned a value other than int (say, pointer to int), a declaration of the form:

```
extern int * bumpcount();
```

would be required.

Data Privacy

In Chapter 3 we discussed the keyword static as it is applied to a local variable. When static is applied to a global variable the global variable is inaccessible from other files. For example, if filea.c contains the source code:

```
static int count;

bumpcount() {
     count++;

}
```

the variable count cannot be accessed from other files. This can serve to protect data from unwanted interference. With this declaration in place, if another file defines a global variable called count, that variable is a different variable from this variable count.

MORE C PREPROCESSOR STATEMENTS

You have seen the preprocessor statements #define and #include throughout this text. There are additional preprocessor statements that have not been used in the programs presented. These statements are summarized here.

The preprocessor statement #undef causes the preprocessor to reverse the effect of a previous #define statement. For example, if program statements appear in the sequence:

```
#define C_FLAG 1

      /* CODE A */
            .
            .
            .
#undef C_FLAG

        /* CODE B */
            .
            .
            .
```

the C preprocessor will replace the token C_FLAG with the character 1 in the portion of the program identified as CODE A. In the section labeled CODE B the token C_FLAG will not be replaced.

Conditional compilation can be performed by using the preprocessor statements #ifdef (if defined), #ifndef (if not defined), #if, #else, #endif. By specifying conditional compilation in your program you can direct the compiler to ignore portions of the source code depending upon conditions that exist at compile-time.

Conditions are tested using the #ifdef, #ifndef, and #if preprocessor statements. For example, the statement:

```
#ifdef identifier
```

is a conditional statement. It is true if identifier has previously been #defined, false otherwise. The statement:

```
#ifndef identifier
```

is true if identifier has not been #defined, and:

```
#if constant_expression
```

is true if the constant_expression has a non-zero value.

When one of these lines is encountered by the compiler the specified condition is tested. If the condition is false, then source lines are ignored until a #else statement (or a #endif statement if no #else is present) is encountered. When one of these statements is encountered source lines are again processed. If the condition is true, the lines between #else and #endif are ignored.

For example, the home_curs function presented in Chapter 3 was written for the VT52 terminal. In a source file, a program could appear as:

```
#define ESC '\033'   /*ASCII ESC */

#ifdef VT52

home_curs() {
     putchar(ESC);
     putchar('H');
}

#endif

#ifdef TTY5

home_curs() {
     putchar(ESC);
     putchar('O');
     putchar('O');
}

#endif
```

If prior to this block of code a line like:

```
#define VT52 0
```

is present, the first version of home_curs is used. If:

```
#define TTY5 x
```

is present, the second version is used. If neither symbol has been defined, neither function is used. If both are defined, the compiler reports an error—the function home_curs has been multiply defined.

Your compiler may also let you define symbols on the command line when you issue the compile command. If this is true you do not need to put the #define statement in your source file. Rather, you can define the symbol on the command line while issuing the compile command. Refer to the user guide supplied with your compiler to determine if this capability is available on your system.

EXERCISES

1. The tree program on page 236 squashes duplicate occurrences of integers in the input stream. For instance, the stream input:

    7 12 2 7 13 2 15

   is printed as:

    2 7 12 13 15

   Modify the program so it prints all the input numbers in non-decreasing order. The above input is then printed as:

    2 2 7 7 12 13 15

   (Hint: add a count variable to the TREENODE struct. In putin_tree, keep a count of the number of times num is seen. In print_tree, arrange to print the num the appropriate number of times.)

2. Rewrite the tree program without typedef statements.

250

Appendix A

Number Systems

A number is an abstraction that expresses a quantity. A numeral is a symbol which represents a number. For instance, the numeral 10 expresses a quantity we generally equate to the number of fingers on both hands.

The distinction between number and numeral is necessary. The example above—there are 10 fingers on both human hands—would be "there are 12 fingers on both hands," if you use the octal numeral for the decimal 10. Both 12 (octal) and 10 (decimal) are numerals which express the same physical quantity.

This appendix explains how integers are represented in the decimal, octal, hexadecimal, and binary number systems; and how floating point numbers are expressed in scientific notation.

THE DECIMAL SYSTEM

We are all familiar with this system we know that the decimal system uses ten digits (0,1,2,3,4,5,6,7,8,9). Decimal numerals are written as:

$$13$$
$$125$$
$$21862$$

The numeral is equated to a physical value by considering each digit to have a *place value*. In elementary school, you learned about a digit being in the one's place, ten's place, hundred's place, etc. Hence, a number like 237 is interpreted to represent two hundreds, three tens, and seven ones. The familiar one's place, ten's place, etc., can be represented as powers of ten. They appear as follows:

$$10^0 = 1$$
$$10^1 = 10$$
$$10^2 = 100$$
$$10^3 = 1000$$
$$10^4 = 10000$$

The numeral 18931 has the decimal value:

$$1 \times 10^4 + 8 \times 10^3 + 9 \times 10^2 + 3 \times 10^1 + 1 \times 10^0$$

THE BINARY SYSTEM

The binary system uses two distinct digits (0 and 1) to represent numbers. Binary digits are called bits. A group of eight bits is called a byte. Computers use the binary system internally because it is easy to represent two distinct symbols electronically.

Binary numerals are constructed in much the same way that decimal numerals are; however, only the two binary digits are used, and the place values are powers of two rather than powers of ten. Thus, the binary numeral:

$$11010$$

represents the decimal value:

$$1 \times 2^4 + 1 \times 2^3 + 0 \times 2^2 + 1 \times 2^1 + 0 \times 2^0$$

This expression can be written as:

$$1 \times 16 + 1 \times 8 + 0 \times 4 + 1 \times 2 + 0 \times 1$$

and, if you perform the indicated multiplication and addition, you see that binary numeral 11010 has a decimal value of 26. This is a way that you can translate binary numerals to their decimal equivalent—first expand them into their powers of two representation, then perform the multiplication and addition.

THE OCTAL SYSTEM

The octal system uses the digits 0,1,2,3,4,5,6, and 7 to write numerals. The place value assigned to an octal digit is a power of eight. Consequently, the octal numeral 3721 represents the decimal value:

$$3x8^3 + 7x8^2 + 2x8^1 + 1x8^0$$

Performing the multiplication and addition, you can see that 3721 (octal) is equivalent to 2008 (decimal). Any octal numeral can be converted to its decimal equivalent by an expansion into its powers-of-eight representation.

The eight octal digits have the following binary equivalents:

Octal	Binary
0	000
1	001
2	010
3	011
4	100
5	101
6	110
7	111

We have used three binary digits (bits) to represent each octal value. This table can be used to convert any binary numeral to its octal equivalent.

To convert a binary numeral to octal, the binary numeral is grouped into three-bit segments, then the table is used on each threesome. For example, the binary numeral 110111001100 is grouped as:

110   111   001   100

and translated to the octal:

6   7   1   4

As another example

110100110 becomes 110 100 110, or 646

When the number of bits in a binary number is not a multiple of three, zeros are padded on the left. Thus:

1101011 becomes 1 101 011

which is padded with zeros to become

001   101   011

and, using the table, is translated to octal as 153.

An inverse procedure converts octal to binary. For instance:

$$274 \quad \text{(octal)}$$
$$010 \quad 111 \quad 100 \quad \text{(binary)}$$

shows that 274 octal is 010111100 binary.

Since conversions between octal and binary are so easy, octal is often used as a shorthand for binary values. That is, writing 75727 (octal) is considerably shorter than the binary equivalent 111101111010111.

HEXADECIMAL NUMBERS

The hexadecimal number system (often called hex) uses 16 distinct digits. They are represented by the symbols 0,1,2,3,4,5, 6,7,8,9,A,B,C,D,E, and F. Since our common number system— decimal—only has 10 digits, six letters of the alphabet are used as additional digits. The decimal value of the hex digit A is 10, the decimal value of B is 11, . . . , the decimal value of F is 15.

In a hexadecimal numeral, the place value of each digit is a power of 16. Thus:

$$72A5$$

represents the decimal value:

$$7 \times 16^3 + 2 \times 16^2 + A \times 16^1 + 5 \times 16^0$$

or

$$7 \times 16^3 + 2 \times 16^2 + 10 \times 16^1 + 5 \times 16^0$$

Hence, the decimal value of 72A5 (hex) is 29349.

Conversions between hex and binary are made in a fashion similar to conversion between octal and binary. Using Table A-1 you see that a binary numeral can be grouped into four-somes and converted to hex. For example:

$$1101110010011101$$

is grouped as

$$1101 \quad 1100 \quad 1001 \quad 1101$$

which, in hex, is

$$DC9D$$

Zeros are padded on the left when the number of binary

Fig. A-1. The Hexadecimal and Binary Number Systems.

Hex Digit	Binary Representation
0	0000
1	0001
2	0010
3	0011
4	0100
5	0101
6	0110
7	0111
8	1000
9	1001
A	1010
B	1011
C	1100
D	1101
E	1110
F	1111

digits is not a multiple of four. For example:

100100101

becomes

1   0010   0101

which is zero padded to

0001   0010   0101

and translated to

123 (hex)

Analogously, the hex numeral 78B4 is converted to binary as:

7   8   B   4
0111 1000 1011 0100

Hence 78B4 (hex) is 111100010110100 (binary).

A hex-to-octal conversion can be made by going through binary. For example:

5   2   1   (hex)
0101 0010 0001   (binary)
010 100 100 001   (same binary digits, grouped in
 2   4   4   1   threesomes

Hence, 521 (hex) is 2441 (octal).

SCIENTIFIC NOTATION

Scientific notation is a method used to express numbers. In scientific notation, the decimal numeral 3278 is written as 0.3278 x 10. The fractional portion is called the *mantissa,* and the power of 10 is called the *exponent.*

Scientific notation can express fractions as well as whole numbers. For example, the decimal fraction 0.005 is written in scientific notation as 0.5 x 10. In this case the mantissa is 0.5 and the exponent is -2.

In C, scientific notation can be used to express floating point numbers (the types float, long float, or double). The basic syntax is:

$$<Mantissa>E<Exponent>$$

as in

$$0.5E4 \text{ meaning } 0.5 \times 10^4$$
$$0.337e\text{-}6 \text{ meaning } 0.337 \times 10^{-6}$$

Note that the E can be in upper- or lowercase.

When negative numbers are written in scientific notation, a minus sign precedes the mantissa. For example:

$$-0.35e4 \text{ meaning } -0.35 \times 10^4$$
$$-0.7e\text{-}5 \text{ meaning } -0.7 \times 10^{-5}$$

Further, you are free to make the mantissa portion of the number larger than 1. For instance:

$$0.05E3$$
$$0.5E2$$
$$5.0E1$$
$$50.0E0$$
$$500.0E\text{-}1$$

are all different representations of the same number.

Miscellaneous Tables

Table B-1 shows you some common character escape sequences used in C, The ASCII character set is shown in Table B-2.

Table B-1 Common C Character Escape Sequences.

Escape Sequence	Meaning	ASCII Symbol
\b	backspace	BS
\f	form feed	FF
\n	new line	LF
\r	carriage return	CR
\t	horizontal tab	HT
\ \	backslash	\
\,	single quote	,
\0	octal value 0	NUL
\xxx	octal value xxx	(arbitrary value xxx)

Char	Numeric Values dec	oct	hex	Char	Numeric Values dec	oct	hex	
nul	0	0	0	dle	16	20	10	
soh	1	1	1	dc1	17	21	11	
stx	2	2	2	dc2	18	22	12	
etx	3	3	3	dc3	19	23	13	
eot	4	4	4	dc4	20	24	14	
enq	5	5	5	nak	21	25	15	
ack	6	6	6	syn	22	26	16	
bel	7	7	7	etb	23	27	17	
bs	8	10	8	can	24	30	18	Control Characters
ht	9	11	9	em	25	31	19	
lf	10	12	A	sub	26	32	1A	
vt	11	13	B	esc	27	33	1B	
ff	12	14	C	fs	28	34	1C	
cr	13	15	D	gs	29	35	1D	
so	14	16	E	rs	30	36	1E	
si	15	17	F	us	31	37	1F	
del	127	177	7F					
sp	32	40	20	(	40	50	28	
!	33	41	21	)	41	51	29	
"	34	42	22	*	42	52	2A	
#	35	43	23	+	43	53	2B	
$	36	44	24	,	44	54	2C	
%	37	45	25	−	45	55	2D	
&	38	46	26	.	46	56	2E	
'	39	47	27	/	47	57	2F	
:	58	72	3A	>	62	76	3E	
;	59	73	3B	?	63	77	3F	Punctuation and Special Symbols
<	60	74	3C	@	64	100	40	
=	61	75	3D					
[	91	133	5B	^	94	136	5E	
\	92	134	5C	—	95	137	5F	
]	93	135	5D	'	96	140	60	
{	123	173	7B	}	125	175	7D	
|	124	174	7C	~	126	176	7E	
0	48	60	30	5	53	65	35	
1	49	61	31	6	54	66	36	
2	50	62	32	7	55	67	37	Digits
3	51	63	33	8	56	70	38	
4	52	64	34	9	57	71	39	
A	65	101	41	a	97	141	61	
B	66	102	42	b	98	142	62	
C	67	103	43	c	99	143	63	
D	68	104	44	d	100	144	64	
E	69	105	45	e	101	145	65	
F	70	106	46	f	102	146	66	
G	71	107	47	g	103	147	67	
H	72	110	48	h	104	150	68	
I	73	111	49	i	105	151	69	
J	74	112	4A	j	106	152	6A	
K	75	113	4B	k	107	153	6B	
L	76	114	4C	l	108	154	6C	

M	77	115	4D	m	109	155	6D	⎱
N	78	116	4E	n	110	156	6E	
O	79	117	4F	o	111	157	6F	
P	80	120	50	p	112	160	70	
Q	81	121	51	q	113	161	71	
R	82	122	52	r	114	162	72	
S	83	123	53	s	115	163	73	
T	84	124	54	t	116	164	74	
U	85	125	55	u	117	165	75	Letters
V	86	126	56	v	118	166	76	
W	87	127	57	w	119	167	77	
X	88	130	58	x	120	170	78	
Y	89	131	59	y	121	171	79	
Z	90	132	5A	z	122	172	7A	⎰

Legend of ASCII Mnemonics

nul	Null		dle	Data link escape
soh	Start of heading		dc1	Device control 1
stx	Start of text		dc2	Device control 2
ext	End of text		dc3	Device control 3
eot	End of transmission		dc4	Device control 4
enq	Enquiry		nak	Negative acknowledge
ack	Acknowledge		syn	Synchronous idle
bel	Bell		etb	End of transmission block
bs	Backspace		can	Cancel
ht	Horizontal tabulation		em	End of medium
lf	Line feed		sub	Substitute
vt	Vertical tabulation		esc	Escape
ff	Form feed		fs	File separator
cr	Carriage return		gs	Group separator
so	Shift out		rs	Record separator
si	Shift in		us	Unit separator
del	Delete		sp	Space (blank)

Appendix C

Answers to Selected Exercises

CHAPTER 2

1. Illegal variable names are:

    (b) 5times   and   Variable names must begin with a letter
    (f) $xval.   or the underscore.

    (g) save!   The character '!' is illegal in a variable
                     name.

    (h) break   Break is a C keyword.

2. Illegal octal constants are:

    (d) 1235   Octal constants begin with a zero.

    (e) 0x03   The character 'x' is not used in octal
                     constants.

6. Illegal string literals are:

    (c) "Hello"World" The double quotation mark cannot
                     appear in the middle of a string unless
                     it is preceded by a backslash. For in-
                     stance, 6(e) is correct.

    (f) 'short cut'   String literals are delimited by double

quotation marks, not single quotation marks.

7. Line 3—lacks a semicolon.
   Line 8—%n is not a legal conversion specifier for printf.
   Line 9—number(0) is an incorrect array reference. It should be number[0].

   Add the semicolon to line 3 and leave the other errors in place. Compile this program. If it compiles without error, link it and see if the linker reports any errors.

CHAPTER 3

```
1.a.  example(c,i,j)
          char c;
          int i,j; {
      }
```

4. Call 1: call by value
    Call 2: call by value
    Call 3: call by reference
    Call 4: call by value

5.c. v,t

CHAPTER 4

1.b. net pay $*=$ $(1.0 + PREMIUM)$;

2.a. z[1]
  b. z[3]

3. i is assigned 13
    k is assigned 1

4.a. true
  d. true
  e. true

5.b. A

6.d. #define ismultiple(m,n) ((m)%(n) ? FALSE:TRUE)

CHAPTER 6

5. The topmost stack element is printed. The top stack element is popped, then pushed back onto the stack. The net effect is that the stack remains unchaned.

References

[BILO83]   Bilofsky, Walt. "TOOLWORKS C/80 3.0 Compiler and Runtime Library." The Software Toolworks, 1983.

A user's Guide to a popular CP/M C compiler.

[DESM84]   "DeSmet C Development Package Manual Version 2.3", DeSmet Software, 1984.

A reference manual for the DeSmet C compiler for MS-DOS.

[DOLO80]   Dolotta, T.A., S.B. Olsson, A.G. Petruccelli, Editors; "UNIX Users Manual Release 3.0," June 1980, Bell Laboratories, Inc.

[KERN78]   Kernighan, Brian W. and Dennis M. Ritchie; *The C. Programming Language,* Prentice Hall, 1978.

The definitive work on the C programming language. A must for any serious C programmer.

[KERN83]   Kern, Christopher, "Five C Compilers for CP/M-80," *BYTE*, Vol. 8, No. 8. August, 1983.

An article that includes time benchmarks and a prototype sort program.

[WARD83]   Ward, Terry A., "Annotated C. A Bibliography of the C Language." *BYTE*, Vol. 8, No. 8, August, 1983 pp 268–283.

One hundred references to C literature. The author provides insightful briefs on the articles.

[ZAHN79]   Zahn, C.T., *C Notes: A Guide to the C Programming Language.* Yourdon Press, 1979.

A formal guide to C.

[ZOLM82]   Zolman, Leor; "BD Software C Compiler V1.5 User's Guide," BD Software, Brighton, Mass, 1982.

The user's guide to the BDS C Compiler. A well-written and informative guide.

Additionally, *BYTE* magazine of August, 1983 (Vol. 8, No. 8) and *PC* magazine of March 20, 1984 (Vol. 3, No. 5) addressed C as the cover topic. Each of these issues contain several articles on C.

Index

Index

OTHER POPULAR TAB BOOKS OF INTEREST

TAB | TAB BOOKS Inc.

Blue Ridge Summit, Pa. 17214